Caribbean Crossing

 Early American Places is a collaborative project of the University of Georgia Press, New York University Press, Northern Illinois University Press, and the University of Nebraska Press. The series is supported by the Andrew W. Mellon Foundation. For more information, please visit www.earlyamericanplaces.org.

Advisory Board
Vincent Brown, *Duke University*
Stephanie M. H. Camp, *University of Washington*
Andrew Cayton, *Miami University*
Cornelia Hughes Dayton, *University of Connecticut*
Nicole Eustace, *New York University*
Amy S. Greenberg, *Pennsylvania State University*
Ramón A. Gutiérrez, *University of Chicago*
Peter Charles Hoffer, *University of Georgia*
Karen Ordahl Kupperman, *New York University*
Joshua Piker, *University of Oklahoma*
Mark M. Smith, *University of South Carolina*
Rosemarie Zagarri, *George Mason University*

Caribbean Crossing

African Americans and the Haitian Emigration Movement

SARA FANNING

New York University Press

NEW YORK AND LONDON

NEW YORK UNIVERSITY PRESS
New York and London
www.nyupress.org

© 2015 by New York University
All rights reserved

For Library of Congress Cataloging-in-Publication data,
please contact the Library of Congress.

ISBN 978-08147-6493-0 (hardback)

References to Internet Web sites (URLs) were accurate at the time of writing. Neither the author nor New York University Press is responsible for URLs that may have expired or changed since the manuscript was prepared.

New York University Press books are printed on acid-free paper, and their binding materials are chosen for strength and durability. We strive to use environmentally responsible suppliers and materials to the greatest extent possible in publishing our books.

Manufactured in the United States of America

10 9 8 7 6 5 4 3 2 1

Also available as an ebook

For Rob, Gracie, and Lydia

Contents

	Acknowledgments	xi
	Introduction	1
1	Migration to Haiti in the Context of Other Contemporary Migrations	17
2	Haiti's Founding Fathers	25
3	Boyer's Recognition Project	41
4	The Marketing of Haiti	59
5	Push and Pull in Haitian Emigration	77
6	Haitian Realities and the Emigrants' Return	99
	Conclusion	119
	Notes	125
	Index	159
	About the Author	169

Acknowledgments

I owe a great deal to the historians who have come before me and who have written so eloquently about the challenges and triumphs of the Haitian people. I hope this project adds another layer of insight to Haiti's unique but tragic place in the history of the New World.

I have accumulated many debts over the years of writing and researching this project. The staff at the University of Texas Interlibrary Loan Services worked tirelessly on my behalf, fulfilling my never-ending list of requested books and newspapers. I thank them for always being kind and patient. Texas Woman's University's Interlibrary Loan Services was also very helpful in locating last-minute newspaper copies.

The American Antiquarian Society, with its collegial atmosphere and helpful staff, still remains one of my favorite research locales. A special thank-you goes to Caroline Sloat, whose early support and interest provided a great foundation. Because of the fellowship award from The Gilder Lehrman Institute of American History, I was able to research in the wonderful newspaper collection at the New-York Historical Society.

My brother, Doug Fanning, and his wife, Carol Blosser Fanning, hosted me numerous times for my return trips to Austin. Inadvertently, Doug played an instrumental role in my development as a historian when he advised me many long years ago to take a history course with Neil Kamil. The class was so enjoyable that from that point forward, I looked to history as a career.

Since that very first class, Neil Kamil has been an enthusiastic and supportive mentor. I learned how to be both a scholar and a teacher from him and will always be grateful for his guidance.

* * *

My colleagues and friends at TWU and UT have been so supportive. During my time at UT, Marian Barber, Lissa Bollettino, and Tim Forest were invaluable friends and colleagues. I am so happy they continue to be in my life. I have been very fortunate to have such a great group of colleagues at TWU. I would like to thank Jake Blosser, Kate Landdeck, Lybeth Hodges, Jennifer Hope Danley-Scott, Mark Kessler, Barbara Presnall, and Dean Ann Staton for their support and generosity. Their interest and suggestions have made this book much better than it would have been without them.

I was fortunate to find Soline Dhaussy, a native French speaker, who helped me translate some key documents.

My thesis adviser James Sidbury has given generously of his time and energy and has become a friend. His patience, fortitude, and kindness have earned my eternal gratitude. As an adviser, writer, and thinker, there is no better model. His belief in the project brought it to the attention of Debbie Gershenowitz, the former acquisitions editor at NYU Press. Debbie's enthusiasm and confidence in the project bolstered me when I needed it. As her replacement, Clara Platter also believed in the project and pushed me to see it in a new way. I believe the book is better for it.

My family understood how big an undertaking this project was, and I thank them for their support and encouragement. A special thank-you goes to my mom. She was the one who provided the beautiful work by Ossey Dubic as the cover image to the book.

Rob, who has uncomplainingly taken time away from his own projects to listen, edit, and coach me through my darkest moments, is one of the most generous people I know. Both as a writer and as a person, I have learned so much from him. He deserves my deepest gratitude. I want to thank Gracie and Lydia for providing well-needed breaks!

CARIBBEAN CROSSING

Introduction

When 120 free black New Yorkers gathered in the African Zion Church in early September 1824 to attend religious services, they received a blessing for a sea voyage that promised to transform their lives, their community, and perceptions of their race.[1] They were to be the first of as many as thirteen thousand African American emigrants who set sail for Haiti in the mid-1820s, taking up an offer of Haitian lands and liberty from President Jean-Pierre Boyer, Haiti's president from 1818 to 1843.[2] Delivering the blessing and farewell address that evening, Rev. Peter Williams, the president of the Haytian Emigration Society of Coloured People and minister of the African Episcopal Church of St. Philips, summed up the motivations for and the significance of the coming voyages. He began by reminding his New York audience that they, "the first from this port," shouldered a great responsibility in seeing that Haitian emigration was a "success." He addressed the congregation as "the pioneers of a vast multitude" waiting to leave the "house of bondage" that was America. Emphasizing that failure would "discourage the great mass, whom you leave behind," and prolong their "degradation and sufferings," Williams reminded the departing Americans that much more than their own destiny depended on their "conduct" in Haiti.[3]

Echoing what other black supporters of this project said, Williams described Haiti as the "*highly favoured,* and as yet *only land,* where the sons of Africa appear as a civilized, well-ordered, and flourishing nation." Highlighting that "good laws" governed there, Williams promised the audience that no prejudice or racial antagonism stood in the way of advancement, because in this "land of promise," they would become "independent and honourable, wise and good, respectable and happy." Just in case they had not taken in the import of his words, Williams warned them that if they failed to take proper advantage of this opportunity, they would bring a "lasting disgrace" on themselves and on "their nation."[4] His message was clear: emigration to Haiti had significant ramifications for the free blacks who remained behind in New York, Philadelphia, and Baltimore.

Indeed, Boyer's offer to settle African Americans in Haiti made Williams's speech possible and made possible Williams's emotional and ideological investment in the project. Boyer desired to tighten his cultural, diplomatic, and trade relations with the U.S. because he understood that diplomatic recognition from the neighboring state was the only guarantee against the retaking of the island by the former colonial power France. He also sought to be included in the developing New World anticolonial coalition led by the United States, known to us today as the Monroe Doctrine. His push for recognition from the U.S. gained momentum in the early 1820s, until it was stopped short by a variety of factors, the most damaging of which was a slave-revolt scandal. In some ways, when Boyer invited African American migrants to Haiti, it was his last desperate appeal for closer links with the United States.

No other nation in the New World attempted such a gambit. Many, such as Bolivarian republics, campaigned for recognition on the world stage and simultaneously received immigrants from the world powers. But none of them parlayed the cultural links forged by immigration to a strengthened recognition case, as Boyer was determined to do.

Caribbean Crossing argues that the emerging ideology of white supremacy faced a major challenge from American supporters of Haitian recognition who publicly advocated for closer American diplomatic ties to Haiti, the self-proclaimed black republic. These advocates pushed the American public further than historians have previously credited into accepting the black nation's racial equality and recognizing its right to exist. In addition, Boyer's own efforts brought the U.S. close to accepting a black nation as an equal twice in the 1820s, until he was foiled by a slave-conspiracy trial and then by the disappointing outcome of the emigration project. Among the participants, emigration was fueled by the stark realities facing their community. In the U.S., the free African American community reacted vigorously to increased discrimination, decreased political and social rights, and a push from various constituencies to find an alternative to the racial profile of the country.

In Haiti, meanwhile, a succession of leaders reiterated commitments to the constitutional goal of forging a "black nation" and pushed international powers to accept the nation on those terms. Boyer—and, in the U.S., community leaders such as Rev. Peter Williams—believed the success of free black Americans in Haiti would make the potential of the nation impossible to ignore. Boyer had won over an important constituency—the African American community—and this community was given a voice by Williams.

Uppermost on Williams's mind as he addressed the New York congregation were the implications of emigration for arguments about slavery and mass manumission. He and other Americans saw the project as countering a common objection to widespread manumission: after we free the slaves, where would we put them? In Williams's final comments, he reminded his audience that "the happiness of millions of the present and future generations" depended on them.[5] Emigration to Haiti resulted from the common desire of black people in the U.S. and in Haiti for the political and social empowerment of themselves, their race, and their nation.

The revolutionary events in St. Domingue in the last decade of the eighteenth century seized the attention of the free black community in the United States just as it had the rest of the world. Even before the declaration of Haitian nationhood, many free black northerners observed events in the Caribbean with a sense of pride and took an interest in the affairs of the island. The earliest surviving example comes from Prince Hall's famous *A Charge to African Masons*, a speech delivered to his Boston African Masonic Lodge. The lodge became the leading black community institution in Boston and later became the Grand Lodge of African Freemasonry that chartered branches in Providence, Philadelphia, and New York City. In *A Charge*, Hall identified himself and his audience strongly with the island of Haiti, foreshadowing black-nationalist ideas of the common bonds of the African diaspora. In this address, Hall linked the struggle for racial uplift to the freedom struggles of Haitians in terms that imply that his audience was familiar with the fortunes of the slaves in the Caribbean: "My brethren, let us not be cast down under these and many other abuses we at present labour under: for the darkest is before the break of day. My brethren, let us remember what a dark day it was with our African brethren six years ago in the French West Indies. Nothing but the snap of the whip was heard from morning to evening."[6] Here Hall uses the uprising in St. Domingue to steel his fellow black Bostonians against the insults they were "daily met with in the streets of Boston."[7] He reminds his fellow Masons and his wider Boston audience (for this speech was published) that not only could circumstances be worse, but they could improve overnight, as was the case in St. Domingue. This message was intended to charge the black community to confront an increasingly hostile Boston environment that had given them freedom from slavery but little else.

The palpable connection with Haiti felt by some African Americans was soon expressed—loudly—in Philadelphia. Unlike Hall's message, however, the lesson cited this time was not one of patience but one of armed militancy. On at least one occasion in Philadelphia in 1804, African Americans responded to racist abuse in American streets with collective violence. During the Fourth of July celebration, in the same year Haiti declared its independence, a few hundred black Philadelphians gathered in the Southwark district, formed military units, elected officers, and armed themselves with bludgeons to march through the city's streets in their own celebration of the Fourth of July. They reportedly knocked down one young man and then proceeded to pick his pockets while threatening death to several others. The next day, July 5, the marchers gathered again, "damning" any white person who came near them and declaring that "they would shew them St. Domingo." By using St. Domingue as their rallying cry, these black Philadelphians showed that the Haitian Revolution had taken on an emblematic role in black struggles against white oppression.[8]

The Haitian Revolution, as it has come to be called, was both a war for freedom and a war for autonomy. If anything, the third war in the "Age of Revolution" was more transformative and bloody than either of its predecessors. Fending off the French, the Spanish, and eventually the English, the St. Domingue revolutionaries achieved independence against fantastic odds, and in a world of slavery, they achieved freedom for its former slave residents. Costing millions in treasure and more than 150,000 lives, the war was protracted, violent, and profoundly transformative—a true social revolution. To understand what moved the slaves to take control of this Caribbean island, the context of the radical period must first be examined.

Without the French Revolutionary principles of liberty, equality, and fraternity that constituencies in the far-flung colonies of the Caribbean embraced for themselves, the revolution in St. Domingue would not exist.[9] The ferment and reinvention the revolutionary principles brought to French society touched off hopes and expectations within St. Domingue's three population groups: white planters, slaves, and free coloreds.[10] The *Declarations of the Rights of Man and the Citizen* and its statement that "men are born and remain free and equal in rights" ignited the free black population of St. Domingue that had been pressing for greater political and social rights in the colony's governance.[11] A group of St. Domingue mulattos led by Vincent Ogé and Julien Raimond traveled from the West Indies to meet with the new National Assembly to argue for equal rights, believing they were entitled to the same legal, political, and social rights as those enjoyed by St. Domingue's white residents. They, too, were free, wealthy, and landed. The *gens de couleur*, or mulattos, made up a sizeable portion of the colony's population, and in 1789, they accounted for 47 percent of the nonslave population of about thirty-two thousand. Most had accumulated wealth through the manufacture and trade of coffee, which grew in the mountainous regions of St. Domingue. Some, such as Raimond, were important indigo planters whose families went back generations.[12] They owned sizeable plantations and employed slaves to labor on these plantations. Many bought into the distinctiveness of color and the privileges of freedom, believing no commonalities existed between themselves and their mostly black slaves. By petitioning for their rights in Paris, they acted to secure the economic and political privileges that by right freedom, wealth, and landownership gave them.

Although many in the National Assembly supported the mulattos' claims, St. Domingue's white planter class resisted any extension of rights to the free blacks, believing it would be the beginning of a slippery slope: "Mulattoes today, slaves tomorrow."[13] They argued that the only way to maintain control over slaves was to enforce the color bar, regardless of free status. At first, the National Assembly members acquiesced to the white planters, but as the French Revolution became more radicalized, the body granted St. Domingue's free population equal rights. In so doing, they opened up a Pandora's box.

Determined to put an end to this metropolitan interference and the destructive forces that Parisian officials had unleashed, white planters took up arms—and armed their slaves—to attack mulatto instigators. They promised that unless the dangerous law was repudiated, they would revolt against colonial authority. Mulattos, for their part, defended against this violence and armed themselves—and their slaves—against white aggressors. By the end of the summer of 1791, however, both groups had a far more serious and ominous threat to contend with—widespread slave revolt.

In late August 1791, a series of slave revolts broke out in Acul parish in the Petit-Anse region, a region with some of the most productive sugar plantations on St. Domingue.[14] Given the region's productivity and the extraordinarily physical demands of sugar cultivation and milling, it was commonplace for slaves in the region to be literally worked to death. Clearly they had little to lose and much to gain with successful raids on sugar mills and cane fields and the murder of refiners, overseers, managers, and planters. The revolt spread quickly, and thousands of slaves from neighboring sugar and coffee plantations joined in the bloodletting, bringing havoc to the entire region around Le Cap. Planters, their families, and overseers fled the murderous and roving bands, seeking refuge in Le Cap. Within days, an army ten thousand strong menaced the town and its inhabitants, and within a month, the slave army had doubled to twenty thousand.

Paris accepted that the crisis in its flagship colony had only grown more dangerous and widespread as warring camps of slaves, mulattos, and whites fought in every region of the colony. It finally took direct military and civil action and sent representatives of the National Assembly, Léger Sonthonax and Étienne Polverel, whom they invested with complete governing power and backed with military troops. These men were expected to regain control, restore peace, and return the colony to the business of cultivation—a big job. Upon arrival, they encountered a St. Domingue torn asunder by internal warfare and by Spanish and English assaults.

Just as the governing powers in Paris had realized what a mess St. Domingue had become, so, too, had England and Spain. Each wanted to take advantage of the turmoil and to place the pearl of the Antilles on a new string. Spain, the colonial power in the eastern half of Hispaniola, pushed into St. Domingue in its bid to win the French colony. It made astounding progress because it implemented an effective tactic: arming slaves. Spanish authorities offered St. Domingue slaves their freedom in exchange for fighting the French army. Two insurgent leaders from the north of the island, Jean-François and Georges Biassou, brought ten thousand soldiers to join the Spanish forces, including Toussaint Louverture, who became a leading general for the Spanish army and eventually the leader of the revolution.[15] To the French commissioners, Sonthonax and Polverel, the Spanish invasion—and their powerful slave allies—posed the greatest threat to the colony's future. They believed their first priority was to save the colony for France. Fearing the loss of the colony to Spain, they decided to grant freedom to slaves who joined the French forces in defending St. Domingue. When this inducement failed to stop the flow of slaves to the Spanish, the commissioners went one step further—declaring all St. Domingue's slaves free on August 29, 1793.

St. Domingue planters—both whites and free blacks—watched in horror as the entire social and economic foundation of the colony was upended. The planters took steps of their own, inviting England to take possession of the island and to reinstate slavery. By 1794, England's troops claimed territory along the coast near Port-au-Prince and, by the end of the summer, the port itself. With the English threat strengthening and the door to freedom perilously near to closing, slaves acted to save themselves and the French colony by joining the French army. That is when Toussaint Louverture, himself a former slave, deserted the Spanish and brought thousands of ex-captives to join the French army. Louverture's army helped to quickly rout the English, the Spanish, and their allies, the planters.

After 1794, Louverture became the most powerful figure in St. Domingue. His charisma, energy, and intelligence allowed him to outmaneuver black, mulatto, and white rivals. In these power struggles, Louverture fought in pitched battles that resulted in the retreat and eventual withdrawal of the British and Spanish forces, the removal of the French commissioner Sonthonax from administrative control of the colony, and eventually the removal of his most formidable rival, General André Rigaud, a mulatto soldier in control of the southern province.

Until 1802, Louverture juggled the conflicting and diverse interests of the remaining planters (even inviting planters who had fled the island to return), French metropolitan authority, and freed slaves to produce a functioning and stable dominion—all the while staying true to his commitment to slave abolition. Increasingly, however, his policies brought into question how free these ex-slaves were, as many plantation cultivators worked under coercion.

During Louverture's tenure, he wrote a constitution, establishing a new labor system of contracts for plantation labor, a new currency, a law and court system, a new tax code, and even a public school system. He even negotiated commercial treaties with foreign powers, effectively managing the colony as an independent and autonomous state. His most important trading partner became the United States under the John Adams administration, which urged him to declare St. Domingue's independence.[16] Yet he hesitated to take the final step of declaring independence, fearful that France, enraged at the loss of the island, would invade. Keenly aware that white allies would be essential to St. Domingue's future, Louverture realized how threatening St. Domingue was to potential trading partners and understood that as long as France provided some legitimate standing and protection, these powers would not isolate the island diplomatically or economically. Despite his supreme tactical abilities, however, Louverture read France's newest leader, Napoleon, incorrectly. Like many others, he underestimated the Corsican's appetite for conquest.

In 1802, Napoleon set his eyes on France's New World empire, determined to retake direct control of St. Domingue and to reinstate slavery there. To do so, Napoleon sent General Charles Victor Emmanuel Leclerc, his brother-in-law, and tens of thousands of soldiers, including veterans of the Continental army and former Rigaud supporters. These mulatto supporters wished to regain control and to oust Louverture once and for all. Neither Leclerc nor Napoleon expected widespread resistance, and they assumed Louverture and his troops would capitulate quickly. Instead, resistance was fierce, and Leclerc, desperately seeking the war's settlement, unleashed "total war" tactics that targeted black and mulatto men, putting to death all who were captured. Even women and children were targeted and subjected to public torture and mutilations.

One of Louverture's generals, Jean-Jacques Dessalines, who was to become Haiti's first premier, also used total war tactics, taking white residents hostage and often murdering them out of revenge for French atrocities. By 1802, however, Louverture's army faced defeat. Many of his generals, including Henry Christophe and Jean-Jacques Dessalines, surrendered and became soldiers in the French army. Eventually even Louverture admitted defeat, surrendering to French forces. Soon after his capture, the French commanders deported him to France, where he died. He was considered far too powerful and influential to remain in St. Domingue. Leclerc hoped French control would meet with no further resistance.

This hoped-for peace never materialized, as many in Louverture's army refused to submit. The fight against the French intensified when news reached St. Domingue that France had reimposed slavery on its colonies of Guadeloupe, Martinique, and Tobago. Soldiers defected from the French army and joined the growing bands of insurgents and ordinary citizens determined to fight the French to the death, embracing the motto "live free or die."

Leclerc continued his barbaric tactics, ordering the systematic murder of mulattos and black families. Mass killings and drownings took place all during the summer of 1802. Dogs, which had been specifically trained to maul, arrived from Cuba to provide added support to the French soldiers, who had themselves been dying in the thousands as a yellow-fever epidemic hit. Unsurprisingly, these practices fueled ever-greater resistance, pushing the remaining mulatto soldiers, including the two future leaders Alexandre Pétion and Jean-Pierre Boyer, who had invaded with the Leclerc forces, to desert and join the revolutionary forces.

Dessalines, as a leading general under Louverture, was little more than a killing machine during these years. His strength and viciousness rallied the diverse groups of mulattos and blacks to unify under his command. By the end of November 1803, Dessalines and his army had routed the remaining French troops. At last, the French commander, General Donatien Marie Joseph de Rochambeau, who succeeded Leclerc after he died from yellow fever, agreed to leave the island. Rochambeau left, however, without signing either a formal peace treaty or a recognition of independence, leaving Haiti and its people vulnerable to future attacks.

On January 1, 1804, General Dessalines declared St. Domingue's independence from France and renamed it Haiti, a Taino term meaning "mountainous," in an effort to remove links to French colonial control.[17] Yet this new name could not erase the profound internal and external problems facing the nation. Internally, the problem of freedom and whose definition would prevail—the former slaves' or the former masters'—continued to destabilize the new nation. Connected to this issue were questions of land distribution, crop cultivation, and labor laws, issues essential to the effective establishment of the new nation. Rivalries between revolutionary leaders also continued to affect the stability of the new nation, as Pétion, Christophe, and Rigaud each carved up spheres of influence. These rivalries not only distracted these men from their real purpose as leaders of a newly formed nation; they cost the nation manpower, blood, and its international reputation as a stable and functioning place. Externally, without a French peace treaty or any other international agreements regarding the island's independence, Haiti remained insecure and paranoid, making national security the highest priority.

Neither Haiti's instability nor internal discord could erase the undeniable significance of the revolution to contemporary thought on the slave system. Scholars have long focused on the Haitian Revolution as that nation's key contribution to debates on slavery and abolition in the Atlantic world.[18] Yet this scholarly attention has had the effect of muting another powerful signal from the Caribbean island: the emergence of a black-led nation and how that influenced the free black population of the United States. When rebels in St. Domingue fought for and won freedom from slavery and colonialism, they directly challenged ideas of white supremacy. When they founded and governed their own state, they again undermined this view of the world by challenging the notion that freed slaves and free people of color were incapable of sustaining independence. With the revolution, they changed the paradigm of possibilities for militant slaves; through independence, they did the same for politicized free blacks. The establishment and progress of Haiti as an independent black nation marked a political and cultural milestone in the African diaspora.[19]

I argue that both Haitian and African American leaders actively promoted the island as a quintessentially black nation. Haitian leaders did so by codifying the concept in the nation's constitution and also by other words and deeds. At independence, Haiti identified itself by color, declaring in Article 14 of its constitution, "Haitians henceforth will be known by the generic name of blacks."[20] All inhabitants, regardless of skin color, would be considered "black," suggesting an open and inclusive black identity. The constitution also outlawed all white landownership, indicating a color consciousness and a desire to keep whites from the island. Around the same time, members of the African American community began looking to the Caribbean island and embracing color as an identifier. This choice, just as in Haiti, was a strategy to unify against white oppression and racism.[21] Yet, in both cases, emerging black identity was not based on an essentialist or biological notion of difference but was characterized by shared goals of unity, autonomy, and freedom from white rule.[22] Chapter 1 examines this migration in the context of other contemporary migrations. Haitians had embraced those goals in their foundational texts and laws, and African Americans increasingly believed that these goals could only be attained in a black-ruled dominion separated from white control. African Americans who ventured to Haiti in the 1820s believed they were settling in a black republic analogous to the United States, a country that offered equality, freedom, and a republican government.

Posterity has not been kind to Haiti's first generation of leaders. Some scholars have characterized these men as originating the economic and political morass into which the country later slid. Leading the first nation in the world to throw off slave shackles and only the second to achieve independence from colonialism, their achievements should be considered in light of the tools available and the hostility of the international community. These leaders were aware that Haiti's independence and nationhood were symbols of racial uplift and proof of racial equality, but they were also aware that world opinion and economic viability were crucial to its fortunes. These early leaders actively worked to bring African Americans to the island as part of their nation-building efforts. Chapter 2 reveals how every Haitian leader starting with Dessalines actively tried to recruit African American migrants. All were motivated by both pragmatic and philanthropic goals. Settlers from America would provide Haiti badly needed workers and market-driven individuals to help transform the subsistence-based mind-set of its people. At the same time, these settlers would be adding to the wealth of Haiti and improving its image abroad. Boyer took this one step further and hoped that by opening up his country to African Americans (and helping to offset the initial costs), he could win recognition from the U.S. By asking the U.S. to accept the quintessentially black nation as an equal, Boyer pressed the government to address racial equality.

Indeed, sectionalist tensions between the increasingly antislavery North and the increasingly slave-dependent South heated up around the issue of Haiti in the early 1820s. Much attention has been paid to the ramifications of this third major revolution on the Caribbean and the wider world, but far less has been paid to examining the influence that the independent nation of Haiti exerted on national U.S. politics and the growing divisions in the late 1810s and early 1820s.[23] Just as the Missouri Compromise was a domestic flash point on slavery, the diplomatic-level foreign-policy debates over recognition of and emigration to Haiti also brought out intensified sectionalist feelings. Conflicting views of Haiti as a dangerous precedent for the South and an important market for the North became entwined in this sectionalist debate. These were issues that Boyer and his supporters grappled with as they pushed for American acknowledgment of Haiti's independence and the subject of Chapter 3. Boyer understood that recognizing his state would put the U.S. on the record as accepting a black people as equals—unacceptable for southern politicians. As Boyer made traction toward support for opening up diplomatic ties, Haiti experienced unprecedented negative publicity, including rumors of its involvement in the infamous Vesey Conspiracy Trials in South Carolina and two other slave-revolt scandals in the West Indies.

Newspapers were central to those who were advocating a change in the relationship between Haiti and the United States and the focus of chapter 4. With journalism in its infancy, these publications were as much a forum for each editor's views and pet projects as they were for news reporting. These newspapers were filled with reports about Haiti and Haitian leaders, including public proclamations, the "progress" of the island, and the commercial opportunities. Even reports that focused on trade offered accounts of Haiti's government and current events as context. Editors such as Hezekiah Niles and Benjamin Lundy and countless others contributed to this public file on Haiti. Niles published *Niles' Weekly Register* and prided himself on the paper's impartiality in an era when newspapers understood their role as representing particular political parties. This stand gave his paper a national and wide-ranging audience. Benjamin Lundy, the most famous American abolitionist in the 1820s, also lived in Baltimore, moving from his native Tennessee, to publish *Genius of Universal Emancipation*. He established his paper specifically to function as an antislavery voice and pushed the cause of Haitian recognition and emigration with it.

African Americans migrated to Haiti because they viewed the nation in many ways as the black "land of the free." Haiti as a black-ruled, constitutional republic offered economic opportunity, equality, and citizenship to all its black residents. By migrating, African Americans demonstrated a belief in a black nation for all the descendants of Africa and understood this move as an important solution to the rampant racism that they increasingly encountered in the United States. In chapter 5 and chapter 6, the individual settlers' goals and experiences are foreground, because—to echo Rev. Williams—they held the key to the success of this project.

American newspapers documented the emigration of African Americans and their initial experiences in Haiti by publishing emigrants' letters to family and friends in the United States—more than a dozen letters in all. Viewed in conjunction with the National Archives' Passenger Lists for New York and Philadelphia, these letters provide a more complete picture of individuals and families. These shipping records account for all incoming passengers into American ports from 1820 onward, allowing for a statistical analysis of the demographic profile of the emigrants. They also show the great diversity of the settlement. The chief limitation of the National Archives' Passenger Lists is that they provide information for incoming ships and register only those emigrants who returned or traveled back and forth between Haiti and the United States. They do not provide a list of all settlers. In addition, no Baltimore Passenger Lists are extant from 1821 to 1832, the main years of returns, preventing thorough knowledge of the Baltimore participants. In spite of these limitations, the lists contain thumbnail biographies of passengers such as the doctor Belfast Burton and the laundress Hannah Quincy. In addition to the ship's last port of departure, the Passenger Lists often include the full name of the passenger, the age, the sex, the occupation, and the country of origin. Not all customs officers thoroughly completed the forms, however. For many entries, only the barest of information was recorded, leaving us with nothing more than "Ann, a black woman with children," for example. Although limited, this source material demonstrates the diversity of the migrants, especially the widely differing social levels and the surprising number of female migrants who participated. The lists also serve to mark the exact time of an emigrant's return to the United States. This information enables some discussion of what provoked the return.

British consular material provides another vantage point on Haiti in the 1820s; this material also informs chapter 6. Charles Mackenzie, the black consul stationed in Port-au-Prince from 1826 to 1828, wrote extensive reports for the British government and kept a journal that was later published as *Notes on Haiti*. In this publication, Mackenzie recorded additional economic data and what Haitian daily life was like during a period when American newspaper coverage of the settlers' experiences had faded. French consuls archived newspapers from their tenure in Haiti beginning in 1825, again providing accounts of life on the island just as American public interest was ebbing. Other sources preserved in the New York Public Library include a series of books called *Recueil général des lois et actes du gouvernement d'Haïti* that records every law ever passed in the Haitian republic from 1807 to 1833. These allow for a greater understanding of the laws, the economic problems, and the changing social environment that the migrants encountered during their residence in Haiti.

Caribbean Crossing in its entirety reveals that emigration in the 1820s was the culmination of efforts among Haitian leaders to gain for their black nation a place at the international table and the efforts of free blacks to push back against discrimination and show the black race as an equal. It also uncovers how antislavery whites and blacks saw Haiti as a solution to slavery's expansion. Finally, it restores Haiti as an important influence on America's nineteenth-century race relations and documents how close Boyer came to winning U.S. support for a black state—a potentially transformative gesture for slavery and race debates.

Black and white abolitionists invested a great deal in Haitian emigration and expected two great outcomes. First, they expected that free black American settlers could be precursors to a much-larger exodus of manumitted slaves to Haiti. Rev. Peter Williams and other black and white abolitionists in the 1820s took those white southerners at their word who said they would embrace widespread manumission if a suitable location was found for these slaves.[24] The second expected outcome was that business-minded African Americans would assist in developing a free labor system on the island that would allow Haiti to compete with the slave states of the Caribbean and the U.S. Abolitionists looked to the island's economic potential as the invisible hand that could once and for all free the United States from the curse of slavery. After winning the long-waged battle against the African Slave Trade in 1808, antislavery supporters had lost some focus. But the Missouri Compromise of 1820 revealed that slavery was strengthening its grip on ever-greater swaths of the United States. Disheartened at how politics had failed to stop the spread of slavery, abolitionists such as Benjamin Lundy turned to economic pressure as a strategy and looked specifically to the free produce movement, an economic boycott of slave-produced goods.²⁵ Nevertheless, because of Haiti's popularity among the free black community and its established economy and society, supporters were confident that the Liberian debacle, which began with dreams of self-sufficiency, would not be repeated.

From the realm of diplomacy to individual African Americans, the emigration movement carried greater political and ideological meaning than historians have previously credited. While the general outlines of the story of Haitian emigration have been known for some time, the motivations and expectations of all supporters—both in the U.S. and in Haiti—have never before been fully analyzed.²⁶ If African American emigration succeeded in earning Haiti recognition, Boyer could potentially have enjoyed the military and diplomatic strength of an ally in the United States and could have focused more fully on nation building. And free and enslaved black Americans could have seen that the U.S. recognized at least some members of their race as political equals.

1 / Migration to Haiti in the Context of Other Contemporary Migrations

When Haitian president Jean-Pierre Boyer spent as much as $300,000 to finance African American migration to Haiti and sent a recruiting agent to the United States in 1824, his deep commitment to the migration project was evident. His commitment became ever more evident to observers when he met the arriving American settlers on the Port-au-Prince docks, extending his personal welcome to them. Providing transport, food, supplies, and housing for up to six thousand migrants willing to cultivate lands in Haiti, Boyer's offer was unique for the time in allocating these resources to migrants.[1]

Although organizations and sponsors called the migrants from the U.S. to Haiti "emigrants," in some senses they were colonists and in other senses exiles. Colonists wish to remain culturally self-contained, retaining language and customs from their home country.[2] Exiles are generally driven from their home or barred from returning. The African American migrants differed from most European colonists in that they were attracted to their destination by its independence from their home nation. But they were not forced to leave; leaving was an act of conscience. To a greater extent than any Europeans since the Puritan "Pilgrims," they sought refuge from exclusion in the home nation in the actively sympathetic philosophy of the new nation. Even as they retained American customs, the free blacks embraced Haiti's constitution, tacitly rejecting that of the United States. The African American emigrants were political pilgrims, and this is what distinguishes their experience from that of contemporary migrants and colonial adventurers.

Boyer was so eager to augment Haiti's educated population and create ties with the U.S. that he allowed these political pilgrims to retain an American identity, even as he fostered the emerging philosophy of a shared black identity. Boyer promised the migrants that they would be settled together and would be able to keep their religion, language, and settlement groups. The original plan was for the government to disperse the migrants to different locales throughout the island in groups of thirty or more. They were also to be dispersed to plantations and regions that needed them; these were also places that were not densely populated, so there would not be competition or too much interaction between Haitians and Americans. Upon the emigrants' arrival, the plan faced obstacles, including the reluctance of the emigrants to follow the plan because they feared isolation, the severe drought and its effect on the prospects of farming and cultivating, and the American ships' propensity to dock at Port-au-Prince over other ports on the island, with the result that the vast majority of African Americans landed at the capital.

Mass migration swept the planet in the eighteenth and nineteenth centuries on a scale not seen since the Mongols. For centuries, nautical travel had been the preserve of the few. Now advances in shipbuilding, naval security, and navigation opened it up to the many. The volume of ships required to transport passengers in these numbers only became available with the development of mechanized yards in the early nineteenth century. The booming slave trade also ensured a constant supply of seaworthy ships and experienced sea captains in ports such as Liverpool and Nantes. Naval treaties slowly reduced the need for warship escorts that cargo ships had previously required. Even without the constant threat from pirates and privateers, the Atlantic crossing was a treacherous undertaking until the refinement of the marine chronometer in 1767. For the first time, navigators could discern their longitudinal as well as their latitudinal coordinates. At the same time, the demise of the feudal system in Europe was freeing up millions whose forefathers had been bound to their masters' estates. Similarly, the end to the period of European warfare that began with the Seven Years' War in the 1750s and raged all the way through the Napoleonic era released hundreds of thousands of conscripts. Tens of thousands of Europeans were suddenly free to leave their homelands to cross the Atlantic and land in U.S. port towns. The 1820s began the first mass migration, with more than 140,000 migrants settling in the United States during this decade alone, as compared to the 250,000 migrants who landed in the thirty-year period from 1790 to 1820. By the end of the 1830s, the numbers quadrupled to almost 600,000.[3] Among these migrants there were more than 200,000 Irish, 75,000 British subjects, as many as 150,000 Germans, and 10,000 Swedes, and as many as 10,000 Dutch. Even though these numbers from 1820s and 1830s themselves were dwarfed by the late nineteenth-century migrations—when in a typical year more than 140,000 arrived—the era of mass European migration across the Atlantic was established.

There were three main reasons for the movement of Europeans: food shortages, economic or social shifts in the home nation, and the draw of cheap land. None of these migrations involved an articulated political agenda as the Haitian movement did. There was no overt welcome extended, for example, from the American authorities to the Irish Catholic migrants or the German speakers arriving in the 1830s as there was from Boyer to the African American community. On the surface, the motivations for the Irish exodus and the German Auswanderung of the same time period bear superficial resemblances to the African American migration to Haiti. In Ireland, both the Protestant and Catholic communities, like the free blacks in northern cities, were increasingly marginalized in their homeland. The Catholic community still bridled under the vestiges of the penal laws that thwarted education and denied them political representation. (The predominantly Protestant Anglo Irish ascendancy and middle class bore the ignominy of the 1801 Act of Union, a piece of legislative suicide whereby Ireland's parliament voted itself out of existence.) Neither the Catholic working class nor the Presbyterian and Anglican merchant class ever cast the act of migration as the response to this marginalization as the African Americans did, however. Many of the Protestant merchants who took up most of the places in the first Irish waves of emigration were leaving a linen and cotton industry crippled by the economic integration with England, a feature of the Act of Union whereby Irish industries competed directly with English industries.[4] They lost this competition, and many sought new lives abroad in the United States. These Irish Protestants, more than most emigrants, were conscious of the portability of their culture. Most still considered themselves colonists in Ireland, tracing their lineage to the seventeenth-century "planters" who were uprooted from their homes in Scotland to settle in northern Irish cities such as Coleraine. The British authorities had charged the planters with "civilizing" the locals through the power of example, if not through that of the garrison. Unlike the free blacks in northern U.S. cities, the planters traditionally excluded themselves from the Irish culture around them. The primacy of the colonial identity is clear from the survival of "Scotch Irish" as a designation of heritage in many American families.[5] Those from the Ulster region of Ireland made up the majority of those who left in the 1800s.[6]

The Irish Catholic community, for its part, had processed the act of emigration as one of exile, or even defeat, going back to the Elizabethan era.[7] The "flight of the earls" and the migration of the "wild geese" soldiers who had supported the rebel earls in their struggles against the Tudors was still seen as the final surrender of Celtic Ireland at the turn of the nineteenth century. While many Fenians and survivors of the 1798 uprising were forced to flee overseas, Irish separatist groups saw the growing communities in New York and Liverpool as staging grounds rather than bona fide offshoots of the nation. As successive waves of emigration gutted the population for a century after the Great Famine, the act of staying became associated with patriotism.[8] Departing Irish immigrants were not "blessed" like those in the Zion Church; they were "waked," as if dead.[9] Even today, as evidenced by the Facebook page "Ireland Abandoners" and debates over allowing overseas voting, emigration is viewed by some in the Irish Catholic tradition as a betrayal of the nationalist cause.

Catholic Irish began following the Protestant merchant class overseas in the 1830s. But the community leaders called on them to stay and struggle against the marginalization. More so than the free black community, Catholic Ireland saw signs of reform in the early nineteenth century. Daniel O'Connell and the Catholic Association kept many would-be migrants from leaving their homeland by involving them in a mass movement. Throughout the 1820s, the Catholic Emancipation movement gained steam, culminating in the passage of the Roman Catholic Relief Act of 1829, which enabled Irish Catholics to represent Ireland in the British parliament. Despite the political victory for O'Connell and other Irish officeholders with the 1829 act, many smallholding Catholic farmers suffered political disenfranchisement. For one of the compromises agreed on by O'Connell and his political opponents was to raise the economic qualifications for all suffrage in Ireland from two pound sterling of land owned or rented to more than ten pound sterling, a quintupling of property levels. By 1837, the majority leaving the island of Ireland were Catholic Irish, with almost fifty thousand arriving in that year alone.[10] In all, 599,125 arrived between 1831 and 1840. Mostly men, these migrants sought work in the lumber industry and canal-building projects under way throughout the northern United States that followed on the success of the Erie Canal.[11] While Irish republicanism splintered after the dispersal of O'Connell's "monster meetings," none of the factions ever endorsed migration as a political act as those who encouraged Haitian migration did.[12]

By the time of the Great Famine in 1847, the British government was footing the bill for Irish passages. This was not, however, because Westminster presented a political or idealistic argument for encouraging emigration, as several groups in the U.S. did. At least during the early nineteenth century, migration was never discouraged outright by European governments, but they rarely sponsored or financed such projects because there was debate about the economic consequences to the sender country and the benefits and the costs of large-scale migration. The British briefly sponsored an initiative to send British subjects to upper Canada in 1815, but the project proved costly and unpopular and was quickly abandoned.[13] While efforts were made by the American Colonization Society to establish a U.S.-government-sponsored migration to present-day Liberia, the organization never gained access to the U.S. treasury and always remained a private initiative.[14] In the case of the Irish, the British government, once it recognized its error in reversing food relief and work relief in the 1840s, sponsored and supported subsidized voyages out of Ireland.

This immigration of the famine Irish, who fled starvation, homelessness, and disease, remains a special case of European immigration during the first half of the nineteenth century. When compared to the migrations of the Scandinavians, the Dutch, and the Germans of the 1820s and 1830s, many of whom left by their own means and migrated mostly in family groups in an effort to advance their economic and social standing, the famine Irish can most directly be compared with the Germans of the 1816 and 1817 movement.

Famine conditions brought some of the largest groups of German speakers to the United States in the late 1810s. Displaced by the Napoleonic Wars and a series of bad harvests, German speakers all along the Rhine River in the states of Baden, Wurttemberg, and Alsace began to migrate in the fall of 1816. Using their access to the inland waterway to make their way to the Dutch coast, migrants left in the tens of thousands.[15] German-speaking migrants had been leaving for the New World since the mid-eighteenth century, when many arrived in Pennsylvania as redemptioners, indentured servants who had contracted to work for a set number of years in exchange for passage money. But the numbers of redemptioners never compared to the tens of thousands leaving in 1816 and 1817. A chronic lack of food owing to a sudden drop in the temperature over the summer of 1816 drove men, women, and children to the U.S.[16] The migration stopped abruptly in 1817 when the Dutch closed their border, refusing to allow more migrants to pile up on the wharfs of Amsterdam awaiting passage to the United States. When many of those who were waylaid found their way home, the news of their fiasco discouraged others from attempting to migrate.[17]

Despite the depredations encountered by the thwarted emigrants in 1817, German speakers living along the Rhine continued to seek ways to leave their homes. In 1822 and 1823, news arrived that the Brazilian government was offering free passage and free land that was tax free for eight years; thousands sought passage out of Europe. An Austrian by the name of Johan Schaffer worked as Brazil's agent to recruit German speakers from all over present-day Germany for the Brazilian monarchy. He succeeded for a time, and by 1830, approximately fifty-three hundred German speakers landed in Brazil's Rio de Janeiro.[18] The emigration, however, was beset by rumors that circulated about the poor treatment on board ship and that all single men would be subject to military service in the Brazilian National Guard. These rumors eventually dampened enthusiasm, and the Brazilians announced that they no longer supported the migrations.[19]

This German migration shares many parallels with the African American migration to Haiti: paid passage, free land, tax-free status, and persistent fears about military service. There was one major exception: the Germans who went to Brazil expressed no explicit political agenda for leaving their country and why they sought a new homeland. Later, in the 1840s, there was a political aspect to the wave of German emigration. Those who followed Franz Sigel and other radical insurrectionaries in the revolts of 1848 had to flee for their lives when the German and Austro-Hungarian monarchies regained the upper hand. This political exile imposed by the enemy was very different, however, from the political pilgrimage made, under no duress, by free blacks to Haiti.

Still later, the nascent Jewish communities in American cities supported indigent coreligionists fleeing the European pogroms through philanthropic groups such as the Jewish Immigrant Information Bureau and the Industrial Removal Office.[20] Like Boyer, Jewish community leaders emphasized the contrasts between the persecution that immigrants left behind in Russia and elsewhere and the—tacit—acceptance in the host nation. But, outside the Zionist movement, the Jewish community never actively recruited migrants in Europe as Boyer's agent did in the U.S. The recruitment efforts of Boyer and those of his supporters in the United States—as well as the expectations they produced—are the subject of the following chapters.

2 / Haiti's Founding Fathers

When Jean-Jacques Dessalines proclaimed Haiti's independence in 1804, he began the process of transforming the former colony into a nation. As a two-product slave state governed by a tiny elite, St. Domingue bequeathed few institutions or foundations to the new nation. Moving this society toward nationhood posed an enormous challenge to the first-generation leaders of Haiti—Dessalines, Alexandre Pétion, Henry Christophe, and Jean-Pierre Boyer—because the issues of land, labor, and diplomatic recognition remained unresolved.

The question of recognition weighed on Haiti throughout the first two decades of its independence. Instead of agreeing on a peace treaty, France and its former colony only declared a truce, which meant that Haiti's sovereignty as a nation remained unrecognized. It also left Haiti vulnerable to future attacks. From 1804 onward, former St. Domingue planters continually called on their government to reconquer the island by military force, refusing to accept that they had lost the island. And as long as France continued to participate in the Atlantic slave trade, the European power possessed the potential to resupply the island with fresh African slaves. Indeed, Haiti remained in the sights of its humbled colonizer throughout the early nineteenth century.[1]

French declarations to invade and reimpose slavery left Haitians uncertain of their security. They also fueled the nation's militarism as each Haitian leader established a standing army of tens of thousands of soldiers to allay security fears. Confronting an international situation without recognition (no other world power would acknowledge Haiti's existence for fear of offending the French), this standing army curbed French or other nations' aggressiveness. The young nation's leaders assumed that once they established and made Haiti a stable, well-regarded, and commercially invaluable state, then diplomats and important allies would rally round.[2] To improve its international status and woo such potential allies, Haitian leaders set to work building the ravaged society into an economically viable nation.

The plantation system was the economic model that Haitian leaders reverted to in order make their nation rich, powerful, and respected.[3] But ordinary Haitians, most of whom were former slaves, rejected this program of growing a cash crop with plantation-type labor. With the leaders of Haiti seeing their hopes for a respected, recognized, and secure Haiti jeopardized by this refusal—but unable to reimpose the plantation labor system wholesale—they turned to the United States and the black community there. Each of Haiti's early leaders looked to these potential black settlers to bring labor, skills, and capital to aid in the building of the Haitian nation, and each looked to the international community for the security of diplomatic allies.

The Haitian strategy of economic improvement through open migration was a new concept in the 1820s. But this strategy became a first principle of many countries feeling economic slack, especially those in the New World, throughout the nineteenth and early twentieth centuries. Sponsored immigrants helped reduce shortfalls in skilled workers. Even the U.S. adopted this approach during the Civil War when the war effort was threatened by the lack of manpower in many important industries. President Abraham Lincoln in his message to Congress in December 1863 pressed for a "system for the encouragement of immigration," stating how "the great deficiency of laborers in every field of industry, especially in agriculture and our mines," endangered the Union's efforts against the Confederacy.[4] Congress acted and passed the Act to Encourage Immigration of 1864, which enabled companies such as the American Emigrant Company to recruit skilled and unskilled European laborers on contract. These contracts allowed the workers to pay transportation costs out of their wages in arrears, subject to one-year limits. Public efforts to push for such laws were being made as early as 1863 when the *New York Times* printed a long letter to the editor that touting the benefits of such a proposal.⁵ As one advocate wrote, "This addition to our wealth by the labor of the children, ... when we count children and their descendants, it would be large, and constantly augmenting, ... at the rate of 125.45 per cent." Not only would these immigrants provide long-term economic benefits to the United States, but European migration would also provide a "cure for all the social evils" that plagued Europeans because it removed their surplus population to the United States, where "population [was] deficient."⁶ Other nations, in particular, Cuba, Argentina, and Brazil, also sought out European migrants to augment their labor pools; Argentina even enshrined pro-European immigrant policy in its 1853 constitution.⁷ For Haiti, however, what appeared to be a simple matter of attracting necessary migrants was complicated by the unique position it held in the world—the only New World nation where people of African descent lived without slavery and ruled their own independent nation committed to the abolitionist cause. Unlike other New World countries, Haiti confronted complex and ambiguous diplomatic resistance as its efforts to repopulate the island was seen by some other nations as an attempt to spread its revolutionary ideas. Particularly in the U.S., the potential that immigrants would bring home ideas from Haiti was seen as a threat to the hierarchical racial order.

* * *

In one of Dessalines's first acts as ruler over an independent nation, he changed the name of St. Domingue to Haiti. Symbolically washing away French control of the island and baptizing the new nation for a new era, Dessalines reached back into Caribbean history to a time before European contact. He used a centuries-old indigenous name for the island, which was among the few remains of an extinct tribe. The Taino Arawak name Haiti, meaning "mountainous," anticipated a new epoch without slavery or Europeans. David Geggus suggests that the choice of an Amerindian name by the leaders was a way to create a culturally neutral—neither European nor African—reference for the diverse population confronting a future together.⁸

The country was divided between rival factions of blacks and mulattos, speakers of French and African languages or Creole, and adherents of Catholicism and Vodou. And these differences in culture, religion, language, and color had to be bridged by more than a mere name change. For some, the animosity that was rooted in the slave past, when creole mulatto masters enslaved black Africans, continued despite the unity shown by some black and mulatto leaders during the revolution.[9] During the last stages of the war, when the French forces turned the conflict into one of racial extermination, unity prevailed. This unity of purpose was short-lived, and the project of creating a nation out of a thinly allied mulatto and black leadership posed an immediate challenge to Dessalines's skills as a leader.

In fact, many mulattos resented and feared Dessalines after the part he played in the War of the South. After 1798, Louverture consolidated his power over every region of the colony except for the South, which was under the leadership of André Rigaud, the mulatto general. Challenged by this rival in the South for supreme leadership, Louverture initiated an all-out attack against Rigaud's troops, led by Dessalines, Louverture's top general. Thousands of Rigaud's soldiers died on the battlefield, while thousands of mulatto civilians were executed after the fighting stopped.[10] Many of Rigaud's generals fled the island for France. When Napoleon sent General Leclerc to reconquer the island in 1802, many of these mulatto generals returned, including Alexandre Pétion and Jean-Pierre Boyer. Distrusting Leclerc's motives and disgusted at the "race war" tactics, these officers, along with Dessalines and Christophe, defected, joining forces against the French military and eventually forcing the French to withdraw.[11]

Despite this sordid and conflict-filled past, Dessalines attempted to address the discord between "Blacks and Yellows" in his most famous 1804 "Liberty or Death" proclamation. In this speech, he spoke directly for the need of these two groups with their different pasts to unite and live harmoniously together. Unity, he said, was "the secret of being invincible."[12] Yet when it came time to write a constitution, Dessalines declared that all citizens of Haiti would be known henceforth as blacks (*noirs*), regardless of the color their skin, placing all colors under the designation of "black."[13] Dessalines's axiomatic view of Haitians as black fell in line with the prevailing idea of how nations were constituted.[14] The new "blackness" of the population has been read as Dessalines's attempt at universalizing Haiti's national identity and breaking down social stratification. It sought to abolish the color divide permanently and to subvert the light supremacy that had prevailed in Haiti's intellectual and philosophical circles and formed part of the justification for racial slavery. The constitution also precluded whites from ever owning land or running a plantation again in Haiti.

To make certain that white landowners never gained access to their former lands, Dessalines ordered the total elimination of all white French residents living on the island, claiming they posed a security risk to the nation. He spared Americans and other foreigners but killed thousands of French men, women, and children. The extent of his ire toward the former French planters surfaced in his "Liberty or Death" proclamation, in which he described white Frenchmen as "insatiate blood suckers" who are "fattened with our toils."[15] In exacting his revenge on the remaining French inhabitants, Dessalines also destroyed a significant portion of the island's skilled population.

That population had already been decimated by the thirteen-year war, in which by some estimates, one-third to one-half of the population had died or fled the island. Another 100,000 to 130,000 were permanently disabled.[16] The revolutionary period also saw the productive fields, sugar mills, and irrigation works destroyed, burned out, or left idle. The large standing army also kept the most productive workers from the fields. Dessalines declared that no soldier could work in the fields, leaving Haitian plantations short thirty-seven thousand potentially productive workers.[17]

After thirteen years of war, habits of work had diminished among the population. Women, who had worked in the fields as slaves, continued to fill that role after independence. They constituted two-thirds of the population, and their labor remained essential to the island's productivity.[18] But they, too, abandoned this type of manual labor, becoming Haiti's small-scale marketers and traders.[19] Without sufficient or willing laborers, the productivity of the island suffered. The production of sugar decreased by 80 percent between 1789 and 1801, while the island's coffee crop fell almost as dramatically, reaching only 30 percent of its 1789 crop of thirty million pounds in 1805.[20] With these levels of production, the viability of the nation and its future economic situation remained in peril.

As Dessalines realized that he needed to do something to improve Haiti's agricultural output, he resorted to the first migration scheme of attracting blacks from the United States. These Americans would bolster Haiti's population, add new laborers, secure skilled manpower, and supply additional military personnel against a possible foreign invasion. Dessalines advertised in northern-based American newspapers and offered forty dollars to ship captains for every man transported to the island.[21] Dessalines also offered to buy African slaves bound for Jamaica from British slavers.[22] Although no evidence indicates that Dessalines successfully implemented his proposals, this project of importing population was revisited by his successors.

Support for a parallel plan had existed in the United States, but whether Dessalines knew of this previous plan is a mystery. In 1801, Thomas Jefferson contemplated exporting rebellious slaves to St. Domingue after Gabriel's Conspiracy. Jefferson, whose ideas of black inferiority were well-known, at first believed that the island held great promise for the United States, especially to southern slave states as a place to exile insubordinate slaves.[23] Eventually, however, Jefferson feared that a powerful black nation in the Caribbean would become a rival and perpetuate a race war in the United States, resulting in the "extermination of one or the other race."[24] Dessalines's actions in the deadly days of 1803 and then again with the French massacres confirmed Jefferson's fears: the United States must be protected from the contagion of the island and its race wars.[25] This extended to trade with the island.

American policy toward the new republic in the Caribbean shifted dramatically once Jefferson became president.[26] American merchants had made tremendous profits outfitting the island's revolutionary army with arms, ammunition, and food supplies during the administration of John Adams. Throughout the 1790s, the United States' willingness to trade without reservation allowed the St. Domingue revolutionaries to consider independence from France. In one year alone, more than six hundred American ships were involved in the trade between the island and the United States. During the late 1790s, St. Domingue's trade was considered a valuable market for American finished goods and raw commodities.

Dessalines, however, underestimated the antipathy he had created among the southern slave owners and their powerful representative in the United States—Thomas Jefferson.[27] Unaware of the new president's animosity, Dessalines wrote personally to the American statesman informing him that Haitian ports remained open to American merchants. Dessalines also highlighted the huge profits that awaited those who traded with the island.[28] He envisioned reestablishing the cozy trading ties that had existed between the U.S. and the island during the late 1790s when the United States became the primary outfitter of arms, ammunition, and food, supplying exports worth $8.4 million in 1796.[29] Jefferson never responded to the letter, and instead of supporting trade, he prevented American merchants from legally participating in the Haitian trade. He did so by pushing a trade embargo targeting the island.[30]

Even before the American embargo, Dessalines had proved to be a poor promoter of Haitian trade.[31] He made trade much more difficult than in previous years and did so by policing what ports and trade goods entered Haiti by foreign traders. If traders disregarded these restrictions, they faced fines of $300 for the first offense and $500 for the second.[32]

By 1807, Dessalines's inability to ameliorate the economic situation had increased his unpopularity among the growing established Haitian elite, which consisted of military officers and newly minted landowners. When he began a new program to place all former plantation lands in the hands of the state and then to redistribute them as he saw fit, he pushed these landowners over the edge. A cabal of landowners and military personnel planned and executed an assassination of Dessalines to defend and maintain their property. Yet despite the unity of purpose in murdering their leader, the Haitian elite remained at odds over who should be the new leader.[33]

Factions gathered around two candidates: one group supported Henry Christophe, Dessalines's second in command, while another group, a mulatto contingency, wanted Alexandre Pétion, the head of the Haitian Congress, to be the new leader. Christophe, the black-skinned former slave, had commanded the northern army during the revolution. Pétion, a military hero from the south of Haiti, had been critical in liberating the island from Leclerc and Rochambeau at the end of the revolution. Battles ensued between the two camps, culminating in a standoff in which each general declared himself the "true" leader of Haiti. In reality, two nations coexisted after the conflict: the Kingdom of Haiti under Christophe's rule in the North and the southern Republic of Haiti under Pétion. After carving the nation in two, both Pétion and Christophe set about establishing control over their respective dominions. In the North, sugar had dominated the region's prerevolutionary agriculture, while in the South, coffee and indigo had been the main exports. In addition to reestablishing production, the two leaders needed to find trading partners and arm the country in preparation for a potential French attack.[34]

As neither leader could renew trading relations with the U.S. or France, the island became economically dependent on Britain. Maintaining trade relations with the island provided great benefits to British commercial interests, which enjoyed a near monopoly of its trade. For Haiti, however, this relationship stunted any economic advantages or bargaining power held by Pétion or Christophe. Even when the United States returned to trading with the island, the British choke hold prevented American traders from gaining a foothold until the Napoleonic Wars, when Britain's attention turned elsewhere.[35]

Despite having access to Britain's insatiable appetite for coffee and sugar, both Christophe and Pétion found supplying these cash crops increasingly difficult. After independence, the means of production remained the plantation system, with agricultural laborers growing the export crops of sugar and coffee. During colonial days, the export economy produced such enormous wealth that little diversification occurred. Few indigenous manufacturers established themselves, leaving the economy completely dependent on exporting cash crops and importing food, clothing, and finished goods.[36] To maintain this system, Haitian leaders sought to reimpose plantation labor regimes from colonial days, believing this was the only route to economic and military security. Ordinary Haitians resented the imposition of this system because it was too reminiscent of slavery, when they worked tilling land and crops that were not their own. They preferred the independence of small-scale farming and trading to the vagaries of the international market. Reconciling the economic imperative of the plantation system with the desires of the liberated workers posed an enormous challenge to Haiti's founding fathers.

Both Christophe and Pétion reimposed labor laws first introduced by Louverture in the 1790s to keep workers productive. Christophe's labor laws were called the "Code Henry," while Pétion proclaimed a "Code Rural."[37] Both labor systems were an attempt to revitalize the export-driven economy that had been so productive—and lucrative—during colonial days. The systems differed in how they were implemented, however.

In Christophe's northern kingdom, the large plantations remained intact, with the state leasing large tracts to members of the nobility and to military leaders. Christophe secured plantation laborers for these plantations by forcibly preventing the agricultural workers from leaving the plantations and refusing to distribute land in small parcels.

Enforcing these labor laws was a group of more than four thousand military police stationed at individual plantations. The police also served as overseers, who watched for idleness among the laborers and used physical means to coerce labor. Instead of cash wages, the workers divided one-fourth of the crop as salary.[38]

Economically, Christophe's system worked, as exports of coffee, sugar, and other raw materials remained high. Coffee exports increased from 5,608,253 pounds in 1806 to more than 10,232,910 pounds in 1810. Sugar production also ballooned, going from 522,229 pounds in 1810 to more than 6.2 million pounds in 1815.[39] Reporting more than $3.5 million in revenue a year, and with as many as 150 foreign ships a year visiting Cape Haitian alone, the kingdom was universally considered wealthy.[40] Christophe was perceived to be so wealthy that one British observer quipped that the Haitian king was "richer than the Bank of England."[41]

In the southern republic, Pétion's administration followed some of the same policies as Christophe. Pétion gave vast estates to many of his cronies who had brought him to power. He also passed a series of laws similar to Christophe's that regulated the work habits of plantation laborers in the Code Rural, and as was true in the North, the workers received compensation for their work. Unlike Christophe, Pétion declined to impose a national military police to enforce these laws. This decision cost the Haitian republic economically.

Although definite figures are unavailable for the republic during these years, its treasury ran a deficit beginning in 1808 that continued through 1812.[42] Pétion tried to encourage laborers to be more productive by creating agricultural festivals that celebrated the most productive laborer on certain plantations.[43] In an effort to gain more money for the treasury and to jump-start sugar planting, Pétion abolished all taxes on sugar exports and increased taxes on coffee production to ten gourdes per one thousand pounds.[44] Sugar promised greater profits, but cultivating coffee fit the economic and labor requirements in the republic: it required far less capital investment than sugar, and individuals could work at their own pace rather than in the regimented factory-like conditions required on sugar and cotton plantations.[45] But coffee was also far less lucrative as a cash crop than sugar was.

By 1809, Pétion faced a dilemma: his efforts to stimulate the economy had generated operating costs too steep for the government coffers. Salaries had to be paid, especially those of the army. Given soldiers' access to arms and ammunition, Pétion could not afford to anger disgruntled soldiers and military officers.⁴⁶ Pétion turned to the only available resource: land. He began distributing land in lieu of salaries in 1809. Treasury deficits continued, forcing Pétion to give away even more land in subsequent years. In all, Pétion disbursed four hundred thousand acres. Maintaining standing armies was an expensive deterrent that strained budgets, and Pétion began looking for an ally to help share the burden.

Unsurprisingly, both Pétion and Christophe sought diplomatic recognition from Great Britain, an important ally if a French war broke out. Great Britain, with its powerful navy, could protect the island. With this added protection, the two leaders could begin decommissioning part or most of their standing army. Diplomatic ties would also legitimize one or the other as the "true" Haitian leader. Beginning in 1808, both Pétion and Christophe sought acknowledgment from Great Britain. Pétion sent an emissary to London to seek recognition but received no guarantees of support. Christophe used a public ploy to force the European monarchy to recognize his state. He sent a fictitious dispatch that stated, "the British Government recognises His Excellency the President Henry Christophe as the chief of the Government of Haiti, and it is determined to contribute its aid to establish its supremacy."⁴⁷ Nothing came of this ploy. Christophe also went out of his way to repay debts to British merchants in 1813, hoping these merchants would help plead his case to the British government. While notices were placed in the *Morning Chronicle* about how lucrative the trade with the kingdom was, no one urged acknowledging the nation's sovereignty. Despite the king's efforts, these machinations brought him little resolution.⁴⁸

Because France continued to threaten its former colony, British friendship became even more imperative. In 1814, French legislators voted to send a French military force to take the island, at the behest of former St. Domingue planters.⁴⁹ This threat kept both Pétion and Christophe on tenterhooks. Fortunately, the unexpected return of Napoleon disrupted these plans, and the imminent danger to Haiti receded—for the time being. St. Domingue planters persisted in their calls for some resolution, however, and the French government, wishing to quiet these warmongers, approached Pétion and Christophe, demanding that the Haitians pay a massive indemnity in exchange for a formal peace treaty.⁵⁰ Negotiations broke down when Christophe refused the agreement; Pétion expressed a willingness to consider such a resolution. Although Pétion never agreed to a peace treaty with France, the fear of such an event pressed Christophe to reach out to British abolitionists—his most vocal supporters—for assistance against such a dangerous détente.[51]

William Wilberforce and Thomas Clarkson, the two leading British abolitionists, began corresponding with Christophe in 1814, and because of these letters, we know something of the king's concerns and agenda. Thomas Clarkson, especially, became both an adviser and an unofficial representative for the king in Europe. Christophe believed that Clarkson held sufficient influence to sway British public opinion toward recognition and pressed him regularly about it in these letters.[52] Christophe's writings show how he agonized over Haiti's future and particularly the issue of recognition; they also show how heavily these issues weighed on his mind. The writings also discussed various policies, including a national education program and the implementation of new agricultural methods, and the cultural life of the kingdom's subjects. Christophe's educational programs pushed English as well as French reading and writing. The king also flirted with making the kingdom's official language English rather than French and changing the state religion from Roman Catholic to Protestant to flatter the British. He contemplated these changes because he wished to remove the cultural legacy of the French and to replace it "with the manners of habits of the English," a people he admired and respected for their antislavery stand, commercial power, and social stability.[53]

Christophe's "favorite plan" envisioned reducing the size of his standing army, but as he noted, without some guarantee of security from Great Britain, reducing the army's size remained out of the question. (According to some estimates, Christophe was supporting a standing army of between twenty and twenty-five thousand soldiers, and he desperately wanted to decommission at least five thousand men in order to return these soldiers to farming, believing they would add significantly to the kingdom's productivity.)[54] In order to reduce the army's population, Christophe needed "the positive assurance" that England would "recognize [the kingdom's] independence."[55] Frustrated by the lack of progress being made, Christophe reminded Clarkson that recognition was both "necessary" and "indispensable" for the "execution of projects in their entirety."[56] Writing on behalf of Christophe was Baron de Vastey, who repeated that

British recognition was the top priority: "Once we have that, the rest will come easily. All our projects looking to the advancement and welfare of our fellow citizens can then come true."[57] British recognition, however, was not forthcoming.

Left with few alternatives, Christophe turned to a novel plan to increase his population: he offered white men citizenship if they settled in Haiti and married a Haitian woman. By offering such a proposal, Christophe overturned the founding tenet of Haitian identity as a black nation for black people.[58] But his kingdom's need for capital and people overcame matters of identity. When this 1818 initiative apparently failed to attract the necessary numbers, Christophe sought help from the British navy to repeople his ailing kingdom. Since Britain declared British participation in the Atlantic slave trade illegal in 1807, British naval ships had routinely captured rogue slave ships transporting slaves. The policy of the navy was to return these slaves to Africa and to resettle them in the British African colony of Sierra Leone or to send them to Trinidad. Christophe offered to save the British the expense of resettlement by buying the captured slaves from the British government for forty-five dollars a person and settling them in Haiti.[59] As Christophe turned to yet another project of repeopling in 1818, this British plan was probably never undertaken.

Understanding the predicament that Christophe faced, Clarkson suggested a version of Dessalines's project to alleviate the kingdom's woes: African American emigration. In his letter explaining his idea, Clarkson enumerated the many advantages that African American settlement would give to the kingdom, including "strengthening" the king's position "at home and in the eyes of foreigners, and of France in particular." This new population would not only strengthen the kingdom in Haiti's long tactical battle against France; it would also give the kingdom practical benefits. Clarkson reminded the king that American black settlement would help him "realize more rapidly [his] project of introducing the English language into Hayti." Not only would black Americans bring with them their language, but they would also bring needed skills and capital because, as Clarkson noted, many of these black Americans were wealthy, some possessing as much as "3000 dollars!"[60]

Luckily, Christophe could turn to Prince Saunders, a native of the United States, to promote his plan.[61] Saunders, one of the first northern African American civic and intellectual leaders to live in Haiti, worked as a Boston schoolteacher before moving to the kingdom in 1816. Upon his arrival, he worked as an education administrator in the king's government. He quickly found his footing as a publicist, helping publish the *Haytian Papers*, a collection of official proclamations and documents from Christophe's reign.[62]

Saunders, because of his American background and ties to black American community leaders (he was married to the daughter of Captain Paul Cuffe, a black New Englander who supported African colonization), excelled at promoting Haiti in the United States. He toured the United States speaking to various African American groups in the Northeast.[63] These talks seemed successful: Saunders, in a report to Christophe, claimed that thousands were prepared to emigrate from New England and the Middle States. Satisfied with Saunders's results, Christophe donated ships and $25,000 to the project. Before the emigration scheme could begin, however, the king died. And with his death, the project to augment Haiti's population and labor systems with American settlers ended too.

Christophe's death was a warning to all succeeding Haitian leaders. Before his death, Christophe had suffered a massive stroke that rendered the right side of his body paralyzed, leaving him bed bound and reflective.[64] According to witnesses, the king spoke of his regrets in treating his subjects so harshly and pushing them so hard.[65] Would Christophe have tempered his iron-fisted rule upon his recovery? He was never given that chance, for disaffected residents of his kingdom took the opportunity of the king's physical disability to depose him, arming and preparing themselves to storm the palace. Rather than submit his fate to the hands of his enraged subjects, the king shot himself as the mutineers closed in. In overthrowing the king, the subjects also overthrew the brutal labor regime that they had endured for so many years. For future leaders, Christophe's suicide in the face of an avenging mob was a reminder of the limits of power and the necessity of foreign support.

Meanwhile, the republic also faced a population and labor shortage. In 1807, following Dessalines's example, Pétion turned to the United States as a resource for populating the island and strengthening his military defenses. Repeating Dessalines's advertisements in American newspapers, Pétion requested that men of color come to Haiti and reminded his audience that the "freedom and prosperity offered" to black people in Haiti could be found "no where else." Pointing to the Haitian constitution—a document that, he wrote, "consecrates all your rights"—Pétion urged blacks living in America to "come and share the benefits" of these laws in a new nation.[66] Whether Pétion succeeded in attracting settlers remains unknown. He repeated the advertising campaign in 1817.

This time Pétion invited settlers "with open arms" and urged Americans to "abandon an ungrateful country" that failed to appreciate them.[67] He described settling in Haiti as a political act that would show "white men that there yet exists coloured and black men who can raise a fearless front, secured from insult and from injury." He also promised the emigrants "little difference in [the] manner of living [in the Haitian republic] from that of the places they shall leave," encouraging a belief that the republic was a sort of black United States that offered its citizens universal manhood suffrage, religious freedom, a constitutional republic, and a maturing capitalist society.[68]

Throughout African American history, economic gain has been understood as a community issue in addition to being a matter of personal motivation. Too often in the U.S., basic economic rights were denied African Americans because of their skin color. Pétion understood this and advertised the economic opportunities in the republic. A skilled worker, he promised, could expect to make six to twelve dollars a week, while farmers would receive two to four dollars a week.[69] He made clear his desire for Americans with disposable capital, pledging returns on investments in "commerce or in cultivation," at "fifty percent per annum." He also assured laborers as well as sailors that they were in "great demand." For "those who have no means," Pétion promised to pay their passages, offering forty dollars for adult men and women and twenty dollars for children.[70] James Tredwell took up this offer and moved to Haiti, remaining there throughout the 1820s.[71] How many other New Yorkers joined in this 1817 settlement is unknown.

Pétion died in the spring of 1818 of natural causes, leaving Jean-Pierre Boyer, his successor, to finish the project. Boyer, born in St. Domingue to a white father and an African slave mother, was educated in France. During the revolution, he had fought against white planters who refused to grant political rights to the free people of color. He also had fought against Louverture and his army with General Rigaud's forces and had fled the island for France upon defeat. En route to France, his ship was captured by American privateers, and he spent time in the United States in the home of New England Quakers.[72] He returned to St. Domingue with the Leclerc expedition and after independence became the aide-de-camp to Pétion. Eventually, Boyer worked as the right-hand man of Pétion, first as private secretary, then chief of staff, and finally the general in charge of defending Port-au-Prince.[73] Upon Pétion's death, Boyer was elected president by the Haitian Congress, ascending to the position constitutionally.

As president, Boyer reiterated the offers made by Pétion to African Americans, requesting that "artisans, farmers, and industrious men of any profession" settle in Haiti.[74] Realizing that the cost of the voyage hindered some prospective settlers, Boyer offered to pay migrants' passage but required repayment.[75] Pledging that migrants who worked as cultivators would find "very advantageous" positions, receiving "from two to four dollars" per week in addition to room and board, Boyer sweetened the pot by promising title to these lands after one year of cultivation.[76]

Echoing Pétion, Boyer assured his audience that Haiti had a wise constitution that "insures a free country to Africans and their descendants." Aware of the American Colonization Society's continued push toward African colonization, Boyer pledged that emigrants would find life in Africa "less easy" than in Haiti and even called African colonization a "less honorable" proposition.[77] Arguing that the guiding hand of "Providence has destined Hayti for a land of promise," Boyer presented emigration to Haiti as more than just an employment opportunity for African Americans; it was sanctioned by God.[78] Despite these attractive terms, these early efforts to attract African American migrants failed to become the mass movement that Boyer envisioned.[79]

Yet the need for cultivators, capitalists, and deterrents to French aggression only grew in importance during the 1820s, and Boyer's commitment to African American emigration grew accordingly. When he revisited the project in 1824, Boyer had gathered support among key constituents in the United States to enhance its success. He would, however, have to do battle against the entrenched fear and racism that Haiti provoked among slaveholders.

3 / Boyer's Recognition Project

In 1818, when Jean-Pierre Boyer became the president of Haiti upon President Alexandre Pétion's death, he inherited the nation-building problems that his predecessor had faced—the costly standing army, the diminished capacity of the agricultural sector, and the stalled diplomatic maneuvers. In a departure from Pétion's rule, Boyer concentrated his energies on securing diplomatic recognition. Recognition could bring security and allow for a reduction in the standing army and the attendant costs of feeding, clothing, equipping, and paying its soldiers. The forty thousand soldiers would then contribute their labor to Haiti's economic standing. This army, by some estimates, consumed more than 50 percent of the treasury, depriving Haiti of vital national development projects such as repairing roads, bridges, and canals; building schools and hospitals; and expanding its merchant fleet.[1] Clearly, recognition was a pragmatic goal for the new president. But recognition was more than that—it would also validate the achievements of the young black nation and give Haiti the standing it deserved on the world stage. Other countries, especially those of the former Spanish New World empire, never faced such impediments to their recognition. Haiti remains unique among all New World nations in that when it became independent, it failed to achieve recognition from either its own former colonial power or from another world power.² This validation was important to Haiti and to its leaders and was a goal for Haiti's early leaders, especially Boyer.

The idea of recognition developed out of the seventeenth- and eighteenth-century wars that enveloped Europe, including the Thirty Years' War and the Dutch independence movement against the Spanish monarchy. Beginning with the Peace of Westphalia in 1648, which set in motion the ending of the multidecade wars among Europe's nations, recognition became an accepted concept in international relations and ushered in the idea of the European nation-state. Hugo Grotius, a political theorist of the seventeenth century, argued the notion that recognition should be granted to a nation to demonstrate that an individual government was accepted within the system.³ Although there continued to be resistance to this concept among the dynastic monarchies of Europe, the American Revolution, the French Revolution, and the Napoleonic era's chaos ushered in a new era of international relations—Europe's monarchs had to acknowledge that these new republican nation-states deserved the same legal status as the dynastic monarchies.

The task that Boyer set himself was formidable. Despite concerted efforts, neither Christophe nor Pétion, Boyer's predecessors, had succeeded in obtaining foreign recognition. Rather than looking solely to Great Britain or France as they had, Boyer sought acknowledgment from the United States, a strategy he believed would help him succeed where they had failed.⁴ Because he had firsthand knowledge of the United States and its interests (Boyer spent time in New England in the early 1800s), the president believed he had the knowledge and political acumen to get the job done. He turned to merchants and manufacturers in the Northeast of America, knowing they would be important allies. Boyer made promises of highly lucrative trade concessions and enormous profits. The American manufacturers' and merchants' growing economic dependence—particularly in northern states—on exporting goods to the Caribbean gave Boyer an important bargaining chip in his bid to win recognition.

What follows is an account of how Boyer patiently pressured the U.S. to the brink of becoming the first international power to recognize the Caribbean nation. In American historiography, Haiti has been characterized as an isolated nation, as a marginal concern from the time of Thomas Jefferson's presidency until

Abraham Lincoln's recognition.[5] What my research reveals is a more vigorous "Haitian debate" that could have gone either way. In the 1820s, some Americans argued that Haiti deserved to be recognized for its republican principles, for its stability, and for its economic importance to the U.S. Meanwhile, other Americans spoke with urgency about the nation's militant influence on free blacks and slaves. The debate about Haitian recognition and eventually emigration were early indicators of the growing rancor and intractable differences between the slaveholding South and the market-seeking North.

From the Haitian perspective, the recognition debate in the U.S. was pivotal. The alternative route to international legitimacy would prove almost fatally expensive. When Boyer agreed to pay 150 million francs as reparations for the property loss during the revolution in exchange for French recognition in April 1825, he signed away his nation's chance of prosperity. The agreement weighed the island down with debts that hindered its social and economic development throughout the nineteenth century. If Boyer and American northern interests had succeeded in gaining recognition from the United States, Haiti might not have been crippled by this enormous and unaffordable indemnity.

If recognition efforts had succeeded, the story of America's race relations would be different, too. In American history, the 1820s is acknowledged by many scholars to be the decade when white racial superiority became entrenched. What the recognition debate reveals is that this racial hardening was not inevitable or uncontested. Many people in the United States understood that this diplomatic relationship carried tremendous symbolic weight. To recognize Haiti as a nation would be to recognize at least some people of African descent as equals and would be proclaiming as much to the world. And this is precisely why the plantation class in the South objected so strongly.

* * *

Boyer emerged as the most important man in Haiti in 1819 when he began reuniting the dominions in the fractured nation. First, he conquered the rogue province of Grand'Anse, a former republican region in the south that had rebelled and gained de facto independence from the republic in 1807. Reports on the conquest noted how Boyer accomplished this feat with little effort, in contrast to Pétion, who had "in vain attempted to subdue" the region for years.[6] And in the fall of 1820, when Boyer conquered the former Kingdom of Haiti after Christophe's suicide, he subdued supporters of the king quickly. An observer reported that he brought "freedom" and "justice" and that his rule was "producing the most happy effects" among the former subjects.[7] The *Newburyport Herald* wrote that Boyer's handling of the conquest "evinces" of his right to occupy "the high station."[8]

Boyer's expansionary efforts and territorial triumphs received further attention and became an enduring point of interest among Americans when Boyer conquered the Spanish colony of Santo Domingo, making all of Hispaniola united under his rule in 1822. When Boyer captured Santo Domingo without bloodshed in 1822, he was taking advantage of the chaos produced by the Spanish American wars of independence that swept much of Latin America in the 1810s and 1820s. Santo Domingan insurgents had rebelled with the intention of joining the Columbian Republic in South America, but Boyer had different ideas. He laid claim to the area, but leaders in the City of Santo Domingo resisted his imposition of power. Instead of immediately acting and sending troops across the border for an invasion, Boyer made public his intentions and announced that a large army would soon march on the Domingans in order "to establish order and tranquility."[9] His gambit of using the media to relay threats of aggression worked, and on January 19, 1822, the former Spanish territory flew the Haitian flag. Boyer succeeded in more than doubling Haiti's size and did so without resorting to a costly military campaign or incurring any loss of life.

Haitians celebrated these territorial gains with a new sense of national destiny and pride. Members of Haiti's Congress, foretold "a new era" that would "fix forever" the country's "happy destiny."[10] Editors of one island publication, *Le Propagateur*, stated, "The situation of the republic becomes daily more prosperous."[11] There was a sense of purpose and expectation that these territorial gains had removed the "dark clouds" that had loomed over Haiti, revealing at last a "horizon" that was both "clear and serene."[12] Boyer's military leadership skills and political acumen had produced concrete results that would translate into economic prosperity for the nation.

These territorial conquests also caught the attention of Americans. After learning of Boyer's conquests of Christophe's kingdom and the Grand'Anse region in 1820, Hezekiah Niles, the publisher of *Niles' Weekly Register*, concluded that the Haitian president was a "considerable politician as well as warrior."[13] Niles continued to praise Boyer for his capture of the Spanish Santo Domingo, stating, "if ever an invasion was a right one," it was this one; it "was both necessary and just." Complimenting the president's leadership, Niles wrote, "there is no king of Europe, with the power that he possess, [who] would use it with the same moderation and justice."[14] And Niles expected that Haiti would achieve under Boyer's leadership "a very respectable rank among the states of the world."[15] A commentator in another newspaper, Philadelphia's *National Gazette*, noted how Haiti's expansion into Santo Domingo, especially "the mild and honorable manner with which it has been conducted, . . . will prove of the greatest importance to the people of Hayti." He predicted that "under the auspices of their wise Chief, President Boyer," Haiti would become "more respectable" and rise "in the estimation of the nations."[16] Persuading these public men of letters that Haiti was under a new type of leader was one of the more important steps Boyer achieved in his recognition project.

Boyer's territorial triumphs raised hopes in American business quarters that Haiti's expanded market (Santo Domingo's population was estimated at one hundred thousand in 1822) would propel the United States out of its stagnant economy. As one Boston newspaper put it, the Haitian market alone could keep American manufacturers "constantly employed."[17] They saw that with all of Hispaniola under one government, the second-largest island in the Caribbean was now a single market. Niles noted that with Boyer at the helm, the island would soon become "a powerful and wealthy nation" that needed numerous American products.[18]

Because of international events both in Europe and in the United States, the commercial relationship with Haiti had become increasingly important to Americans in the late 1810s and 1820s.[19] American manufacturing in the northern states had taken off in the 1800s and 1810s, helped by Jefferson's temporary ban on foreign trade in 1806. His embargo stimulated American industry in cotton, wool, and iron manufacturing.[20] Great Britain had been kept busy by the Napoleonic Wars in Europe, allowing American industries to flourish in isolation. Once peace returned to Europe in 1815, Great Britain's attention refocused on the lucrative American market, leaving the nascent American manufacturing sector struggling to compete against the cheaper and more efficiently produced British goods.[21] Many American textile factories went bust, and more than half of that industry's workforce was left unemployed. Even when the United States passed protective tariffs in 1816, they proved futile against the British onslaught. To make matters worse, in 1817, British economic policies closed many Caribbean ports to American trade as part of the British Corn Laws, leaving American commercial interests with few easily accessible overseas markets. To survive, American industrialists and merchants were forced to seek out new overseas markets. The only market that could compare to the British West Indies in terms of accessibility or spending power was Haiti.[22]

The situation became even more desperate with the Panic of 1819, an unprecedented economic downturn.[23] The Panic left five hundred thousand people nationwide out of work. In New York, Baltimore, and Philadelphia alone, fifty thousand people were either unemployed or irregularly employed. Farmers also felt the effects, as commodity prices dropped 30–50 percent.[24] As one American put it in 1822, "Last year we talked of the difficulties of paying for our lands; this year the question is, how to exist."[25]

In the 1820s, the opening up of new markets became imperative for the economic survival of American society, and Haiti's expanding consumer market was looking better and better. Even before the annexation of Santo Domingo to Haiti, the value of American exports sold to the island increased by seventeenfold between 1817 and 1820 (from $130,000 to $2.2 million). This was during a period when world commodity prices fell dramatically.[26] Though Haiti's trade made up only 5 percent of all American exports, the turbulent economic situation in the U.S. during these Panic years meant any increase in overseas markets was greatly valued.[27] As one American observer wrote of the country's relationship with Haiti, American exports to Port-au-Prince were of such "magnitude" that the U.S. "government and citizens" needed to realize "the importance of the commerce of our country with this island."[28]

Niles highlighted how perfectly Haiti complemented American needs and how it was in the position to influence American recovery efforts. He used his influence to give sustained coverage to the importance of Haiti's trade. He wrote in his March 23 edition, "trade with these blacks is more important, in amount, to us, than that of many countries in whom we have highly dignified ministries and agents."[29] He continued to make the point when he explained about Haiti's trade, "[It is] more valuable to us than any other—taking off a large amount of the products of our fields and forests, and latterly receiving considerable quantities of our manufacturers."[30] As another newspaper pointed out, not only did Haiti take American manufacturing surpluses, but the island bought large quantities of American fish, wheat, and, rice.[31] Editors and readers of the *Boston Patriot*, *Poulson's American Daily Advertiser* (Philadelphia), and the *Newburyport Herald* echoed Niles's sentiments on how this market could serve American manufacturers.[32]

Because of the increased importance of Haiti to American merchants, they sought the best possible trading relationship. These American merchants began to demand that Haiti be recognized and used domestic newspapers to publicize these calls. This recognition, they argued, would give merchants greater profits because of the more favorable trading duties. Americans paid 12 percent duties on goods, while British traders and merchants paid 7 percent. (The lower duty the British enjoyed was a holdover from the days when Great Britain monopolized the trade.)[33] American merchants, because of their greater numbers and high volume of trade with the island, wanted Boyer to cut the duty they paid by almost 50 percent to match the British rate.[34] For Boyer, however, without some sort of diplomatic effort by the United States, there was little reason to consider lowering the tariffs.

Despite this situation, American administrations officially ignored the island's commercial links and diplomatic status. A reader of the *Boston Centinel* complained that "the apathy and indifference of the American government" meant that the Haitian trade was "left to take care of itself."[35] In a letter published in *Poulson's*, another commentator urged "statesmen, merchants and philanthropists" to act with justice toward Haiti and to acknowledge that nation's right to independence.[36] Comments like these could be found in newspapers in many northern cities.

Southern slave owners bridled at the prospect of a closer diplomatic and economic relationship between the island and the United States, and they demanded their interests be taken into account. The editor of *United States Gazette* cautioned that any change in diplomatic status would damage "the interests of the south and the slave holding states." He urged the United States to remember that it must "consult general rather than individual interests."[37] Senator Thomas Hart Benton of Missouri demonstrated the southern position on this debate: "Our policy . . . has been fixed, Mr. President, for three and thirty years. We trade with [Haiti], but no diplomatic relations have been established between us. We purchase coffee from her, and pay her for it, but we interchange no consuls or ministers, . . . [as] the peace of eleven [slave-owning] states will not permit the fruits of a successful negro insurrection to be exhibited among them."[38] An article in the *Baltimore Patriot* crystallized two sides of the question: "Hayti, under its present circumstances, must be and in fact is viewed by the Southern Planters, with great anxiety; while its valuable commerce renders it an object of interest to our merchants."[39] How were these two contradictory positions regarding Haiti to be resolved?

Published in Baltimore, the most southern of the North's cities, the *Baltimore Patriot* was well positioned to make such assessments. Hezekiah Niles, who also lived in Baltimore, understood the North-South split clearly.[40] Aware that this split could waylay commercial and diplomatic relations, Niles used his direct access to readers to argue that the interest of the people of the U.S. with Haiti was less "sectional" than "some would make it out to be."[41] He pointed out that southerners' economic self-interests were as tied up with the Haitian trade as northerners' were. For example, he argued, the Caribbean trade boosted prices of flour, an important cash crop in the Upper South.[42] Niles would have been very familiar with the flour industry, as Baltimore was becoming the primary port for this commodity.[43]

Even as men such as Niles argued that recognition was good for all Americans, Boyer had to contend with interest groups in Haiti that opposed his course of action. That is partly because Boyer used a tactic that was to become commonplace among small countries in the twentieth century: he made his country a more attractive place for foreigners to do business. He did this by honoring debts incurred during Pétion's administration, paying one American merchant $60,000.[44] He also gave foreign merchants more options for debt collecting, which enabled them to use the island's court system to force Haitians to pay their loans. Boyer understood that merchants were pivotal allies in the battle for recognition and accommodated them as much as he dared.

Boyer also made traveling to Haiti easier for merchant captains. As W. Jeffrey Bolster's work has revealed, during Pétion's administration, black sailors were able to desert from ships with impunity, claiming abusive employment situations. Throughout Pétion's presidency, Haiti's courts ruled in favor of the black sailors' rights.[45] Yet during Boyer's presidency, he occasionally reversed the courts' decision, ruling in favor of captains.[46] Because of these and other changes, the president was "much esteemed" by the owners of these merchant ships.[47]

Boyer's initiatives brought condemnation and praise from different sections of the Haitian populace. Many in the nation's intellectual class, such as publishers and writers, supported the president's efforts because they saw his policies having the desired effect of enhancing Haiti's international reputation. After reading a Boston newspaper's report on Haiti and the commercial advantages to Americans who traded there, the editor of the Haitian publication *Le Propagateur* predicted, "[Soon] our republic will stand among the independent governments of the world."[48] The writer implied that the protrade policies had as much to do with recognition as they did with economic development. Not everyone shared *Le Propagateur*'s impression of Boyer's protrade policies, however. Some opponents employed sabotage to make their views known, while others—to their peril—publicly condemned Boyer's policies.

The first tactic made its appearance at noon on August 15, 1820, when "a great fire" started near the center of Port-au-Prince. The blaze incinerated between four and five hundred buildings, most of them merchants' homes and warehouses. Damage estimates ran between $3 million and $4 million. The published newspaper reports portrayed the fire as arson designed to burn out foreign merchants.[49] Boyer, faced with the angry condemnation and possible economic retaliation from these merchants, sought to placate them.[50] He removed for five years the patent taxes that foreign merchants were required to pay as well as duties on building materials. This was a considerable and expensive concession since each foreign merchant paid $1,600 a year into the Haitian treasury.[51] Evidently, this gesture angered his opponents even more, since another fire broke out in December 1822, in the exact same location as the 1820 fire. This, too, was reportedly "the work of an incendiary." The second fire caused losses of $4 million to foreign merchants.[52]

The burning of cities, especially Port-au-Prince and Le Cap, had been employed by rebels during the Haitian Revolution and was a well-known tactic in expressing opposition on the island. Boyer also encountered opposition to his policies in political circles. In 1822, political opponents challenged the president when Felix Darfour, a member of Haiti's elite, spoke to an assembled meeting of the Haitian Congress. Darfour railed against the president's trade concessions to foreigners and accused Boyer of selling "the country to the whites."[53] The official report published in *Le Telegraphe*, another Haitian publication, insisted that Darfour acted treasonously and was "agitating a conspiracy."[54] Boyer acted quickly: he removed all of Darfour's supporters within the Congress from government duty and banished them from Port-au-Prince. Eventually, Darfour was executed for seditious behavior.[55]

Because the incident received so much coverage in American newspapers,[56] Benjamin Lundy accused opponents of Haiti of using it to argue that black people were "inferior to the whites" and that "the government of Hayti" was "despotic."[57] Lundy, editor of the *Genius of Universal Emancipation* and a leading American abolitionist of the 1820s, was disgusted at the denigration of the island nation that he perceived in the coverage. He reminded his audience that the critics of Haiti were "republican advocates of slavery," who had little grounds to throw stones. Lundy admitted that the government of Haiti may have acted rashly in the Darfour case but stated that overall the "principles of liberty" were established there.[58] Lundy later became a staunch supporter of Haitian emigration.

Despite setbacks to Haiti's international reputation with the incidents of arson directed at merchants and the Darfour situation, Boyer and American supporters remained optimistic about recognition. The *Boston Centinel* opined, "the prejudices against the [Haitians] are fast wearing away, and the day, we trust, is not far distant when the United States will acknowledge their independence."[59] Boyer and his supporters appeared on the brink of success when a writer for the *Newburyport Herald* predicted that President James Monroe's next message to Congress would "recommend the recognition of the Government of Hayti."[60] This recognition was all that Boyer had hoped for and was the potential culmination of all of his efforts. But in fact, Monroe recognized the first of the South American countries to win independence from Spain: Argentina and then Columbia. He did so without mentioning Haiti or its recognition altogether.

Commentators in both the United States and Haiti immediately voiced their opposition to Monroe's diplomatic slap. One writer, who used the pen name "Howard," objected to the United States' double standard, arguing that the new nations of South America were not as permanently settled as Haiti was: "if we adhere to the principles which governed us in our conduct towards the nations in our Southern hemisphere, how can we without our acknowledgment of the Republic of Hayti?" Howard explained that Haiti possessed "superior claims" because "the government has been permanently established: the people are governed by laws impartially administered and promptly executed; no foreign nation influences or controls the government; in their dealing with other nations, they manifest a liberal and just policy; and the nation has abundant resources to maintain its independence."[61] Boyer wrote that it was an "outrage done to the Haytian character" that certain powers acknowledged the South American states' independence, "while they pass over" Haiti's rights. Boyer complained that this was a "humiliating silence."[62]

Feeling that the time was right for direct action, Boyer sent a letter of appeal to Secretary of State John Quincy Adams. He asked how the administration could refuse Haiti the justice that was its due and reminded Adams that the United States had "in another epoch found themselves in the same situation and felt the same need" for recognition.[63] Boyer also appealed to the United States as a trading partner "who exchange[s] the products of [its] soil" to "feel the necessity of acknowledging the Independence of the Queen of the Antilles."[64] The phrase "Queen of the Antilles" was an old sobriquet for St. Domingue, an epithet that recalled its reign as the most productive and richest colony in the Caribbean, if not in the world.

Advocates of recognition echoed these arguments, writing that Haiti's progress as a nation, its stability, its republican sensibilities, and its American-like revolutionary heritage warranted its acknowledgment. O. L. Holly delivered a Fourth of July speech in which he exhorted his audience to consider the Haitian Revolution "without prejudice." He also praised the citizens of the island: "[Despite] the obstacles thrown in their way by the jealous pride of other nations, they have confirmed their sovereignty. They have cultivated successfully the arts of peace, as well as war; commerce has prospered with them; and they have already done much towards provid[ing] for their own education and moral advancement."[65] The unspoken sticking point was race. To convince the American public that the island deserved to be treated like any other independent and sovereign state was to assail the prevailing conventional wisdom of white superiority. The liberated Howard believed that the fact that the Haitian people's skin color was "a few shades darker than" that of white Americans should have had no bearing on recognition. He chastised supposedly liberal Republicans "who profess to believe in the principles of that immortal instrument, the Declaration of Independence," for so unworthy a prejudice. Asserting that "the Almighty, in his Providence" had already "granted Independence to Hayti," Howard argued that the United States should do the same.[66] Other supporters pointed to the island's constitutional government, "of which the most enlightened nation of *white men* might be proud."[67] How these public statements affected Adams's view on recognizing Haiti remains unknown.[68] The Monroe administration did seek to improve trade relations with Haiti by sending Andrew Armstrong, the commercial agent to the island, to negotiate trade duties with Boyer in January 1824.[69]

In addition to the disappointment over the Monroe administration's recognition of some of the newly independent South American countries, Boyer and advocates for Haiti received another setback: the news of the Denmark Vesey slave conspiracy in South Carolina. In July 1822 in Charleston, South Carolina, evidence of a revolt planned against the white populace by a diverse group of rebels, free blacks, and enslaved people was uncovered (or, contemporary historians have argued, was created). The authorities acted quickly and apprehended the conspiracy's alleged ringleader within hours of the investigation's onset, naming the organizer as Denmark Vesey, a free black fifty-five-year-old carpenter. By the investigation's conclusion, thirty free and enslaved blacks had died on the gallows, and numerous other coconspirators were banished from the state.

Fatally, for recognition advocates, much of the conspiracy theory revolved around Haiti. During the trial, accusers outlined an elaborate and detailed plot that even featured Boyer as an active agent who had planned to provide ships and give refuge to the rebels in Haiti. Michael P. Johnson, a historian who has studied the Charleston conspiracy, concludes that there was indeed a conspiracy in Charleston—it was among the white prosecutors who relentlessly sought out and concocted evidence against would-be conspirators.[70] Whether or not a conspiracy existed in Charleston in 1822 to destroy the slave system is beyond the scope of this discussion. What is of interest is the active role ascribed to Boyer and Haiti by the white community. Why did the Charleston community fit the Caribbean island into its conspiracy?

Haiti was also on trial in the Vesey case because the island was also judged a threat to slavery. This idea extended far beyond Charleston and continued to be an issue that Haiti confronted in its diplomatic and economic relations throughout the nineteenth century. Although there were certainly many factors aligned against Haiti's succeeding in gaining diplomatic recognition from the United States, the hysteria in Charleston added to the challenges and helped stem the rising tide of favorable opinion toward Haiti. As the editors in the *National Intelligencer* wrote, "It appears strange to us that the idea [of Haitian recognition] should be entertained and pressed, at the time when one the southern states is just developing and counteracting a negro plot which involved general massacre and misrule."[71] Is this strange, or is this evidence of southerners using the Vesey conspiracy to end public discussions of Haitian recognition?

Haiti's supporters could do little but reiterate that the island played no part in the Charleston slave conspiracy, as a *Boston Patriot* article in September 1822 and a *Boston Commercial Gazette* article in late August did. The *Gazette* writer repudiated the role that

President Boyer supposedly played in South Carolina and believed that the Haitian-Vesey connection only showed "the groundless jealousy of the slave holding states against the free government of Hayti." The writer continued to defend Haiti by stating, "it is neither in the interest or the inclination of the Haytiens to disturb the peace of any government, whether they possess slaves or not." The *Patriot* writer simply asked the United States to take "immediate measures" toward recognizing Haiti's independence.[72]

Boyer attempted to offset this bad publicity by appealing to the northern economic interest groups that had been so gung ho on Haitian recognition before the Vesey trials. He asked "friends of liberty in the United States" who "interest themselves particularly in the fate of the Haytians" to continue to "exercise a happy influence upon the public opinion."[73] Although at least one newspaper continued to lobby for the nation's claim to recognition, the argument was essentially over.[74] Even Hezekiah Niles counseled the United States to take a cautious approach, in his edition of September 27, 1822.[75]

The spate of bad publicity did not end with the South Carolina incident. Boyer became a bogeyman whom supporters of slavery invoked as a "black menace," personifying the dangers of abolition. White southerners continued to associate Boyer with other slave rebellions in the region, while colonists in Martinique and Jamaica claimed that slave uprisings on their islands were instigated and supported by Haitians.[76] Boyer assured the international community that neither he nor any individual Haitian provoked these conspiracies, and he issued a proclamation stating that his nation had "no participation in the disturbances that have taken place in the West India Islands."[77]

In an effort to forestall accusations of supporting neighboring slave revolts, Boyer was forced to isolate his nation by declaring an embargo. This embargo separated Haiti from all its Caribbean neighbors, as well as from the states of North and South Carolina.[78] The law forbade "the entry of all vessels, either from Europe, or South or North America" into Haitian ports if they had "touched at any other Island in the West Indies."[79] As one observer noted in *Poulson's*, this law showed in "the most explicit manner, that the Haytien government does not wish to interfere in the rights of others, or to meddle, in any way, with the concerns of the neighboring islands disproving all the false assertions which have been made, that Hayti has lent its aid or influence in exciting commotions among slaves or other islands, or in the southern States." The report ended with high praise for the law and stated that Boyer could not have adopted "a more salutary measure."[80]

After the summer of 1822, Boyer's recognition campaign lost much of its support.[81] No mention was made of the island during Monroe's 1823 address to Congress, which included an articulation of the famous Monroe Doctrine asserting American primacy in the hemisphere. Boyer felt the slight and sent expressions of his displeasure to American newspapers to print. These publications, however, did not print the supportive commentary that had previously accompanied such statements.[82]

With Boyer's support eroding, he changed tactics. Having lost northern public support, he stopped pushing directly for recognition from the United States. Boyer's quest to bring the United States and Haiti closer continued, however, and he sought out other means of appeal by revising an old idea—of offering Haiti as an emigrant destination for African Americans. Given a clearer understanding of how the different interests in the United States clashed over their nation's relationship to Haiti, Boyer believed that opening his nation as a relocation site for African Americans would mute opposition to recognition. By serving white northerners' desires for an increase in trade and some southerners' hope for a destination to which they could deport freed slaves, Boyer anticipated success.[83]

In Boyer's public offer of the proposal, he made the "win-win" aspects clear to American audiences. First, he addressed the northerners' interests. He noted that "the more consumers" that "a manufacturing state" such as the United States could gain elsewhere, the better it would be. In sending hundreds of thousands of American settlers, a population with the "manners, taste, language and impress of North American character," Boyer predicted that American goods would obtain "greater preference" in Haiti and thus further augment the trade between the two nations.[84] His appeal, however, did not end there. He pointed out that emigration would also whiten America.[85] Emigration, Boyer argued, would foster this goal by withdrawing such large numbers of black people that it would "bring into more active and successful exercise, the arts, professions and employment of a numerous class of ... white citizens."[86]

Boyer then addressed southern interests. He argued that the migration of enslaved Americans would benefit white southerners by providing them a method of freeing their slaves without any "dread of future consequence." He even used the recent scare of the Denmark Vesey conspiracy to remind his audience that as "long as the United States bears within its bosoms a population of two million, strangers to its general interests as well as to the very existence of the country, ... it slumbers upon the brink of a volcano, where the explosion will be the more appalling, [the] ... longer [it is] retarded." Boyer assured his audience that the removal of African Americans to Haiti would root out the "political cancer" that was preying on the nation's "vitals"; it would also establish forever America's "happiness, glory, and independence."[87] This bright future, Boyer implied, could only be achieved by making his nation the destination for African Americans. Appealing to American economic interests had failed, so Boyer offered Haiti as a release valve for its racial tensions. Not only could America export its goods to Haiti, Boyer argued, but it could also export its race problem.

Although Boyer's initial efforts to gain recognition had been thwarted, his grasp of American social and political issues provided him another chance for achieving recognition—African American emigration. He understood how important African American removal was to most American constituents and how this majority could force reluctant reformers to the table. How realistic was this possibility? As William Freehling has so brilliantly articulated in his work, the South had increasingly become splintered, with Upper South planters hoping for some sort of solution to slavery and Deep South planters holding back and eventually moving into a defensive mode.[88] But that posture may have been harder to justify if emigration succeeded, and this is what Boyer gambled on in his second bid for recognition. Assisted by potential settlers, abolitionists, and disgruntled American Colonization Society members, Boyer seized another opportunity to pursue Haiti's recognition. When Boyer advertised Haiti as an emigrant destination for free and enslaved African Americans in 1824, he was capitalizing on the positive media attention that Haiti had received in American newspapers. In this 1824 offer, he calculated that his nation could no longer be ignored diplomatically by the government of the U.S.

4 / The Marketing of Haiti

In the 1820s, debate in America's public square returned again and again to the linked questions of slavery and race. Several groups came forward with comprehensive "solutions" to the perceived problem of managing slave and free black populations, most famously the American Colonization Society (ACS). This group envisioned African colonization as a sort of safety valve for America's race problem, whereby excess black people could be siphoned off, reducing tensions between the races and between northern and southern states.[1] The ACS colony in Liberia began to fail as soon as the first settler made landfall in 1821, and yet the society's ideas retained their currency throughout the ensuing decade. The ACS also inspired a rival, and parallel, lobby: those white Americans who supported Haitian emigration.

A comparable media campaign advocating migration was under way in Great Britain and in the areas that make up present-day Germany. According to the leading historians of these migrations, the media played a crucial role in pushing migration to the top of the public imagination. It also helped transform public opinion toward a positive view. In the 1820s, opinion shifted in both countries from migration as a blight that robbed society of the "best and the brightest" to a worthy pursuit that "should be considered seriously" by the citizenry.[2] This perspective was in direct contrast to the views held in the 1810s. The change was a result of the shift in economic conditions in Europe. In Germany, after the fiasco that many would-be migrants encountered in the 1816 mass migration, when many became marooned in the Netherlands without money or food while waiting for passage to America, the public initially turned away from the idea of the United States as a possible refuge. The idea regained currency among the public when travel narratives began to appear and newspapers began to publish these accounts as well. In all, more than 150 travel narratives were written between 1827 and 1856. One such narrative, Gottfried Duden's *Report on a Journey to the Western States of North America* (1829), has been characterized by German historians who study emigration as "unquestionably the most popular and influential description of the United States to appear during the first half of the century."[3] Duden's influence was so great that tens of thousands of German speakers arrived in southern Missouri, expecting to follow in Duden's footsteps and farm land along the Missouri River.

For the British, there was no one media sensation like Duden's that helped fuel migration. Instead, there was an "explosion of information and commentary about America."[4] The New World had been in the British psyche since the seventeenth century, but the sheer numbers leaving and the sustained media coverage made the nineteenth-century emigration movement unique. Travelers' accounts, newspapers, pamphlets, settlers' accounts, and guides such as *Chamber's Information*, *Counsel for Emigrants*, and *Advantages to Emigration* all fueled public curiosity about the U.S. and emigration in general. According to one historian's assessment, there was a sense of the "tides of emigration" drawing people to the former British colony.[5] This became a cause for concern in the 1810s, and the British government pushed these tides toward British North America through assistance programs, comparable to the Haitian incentives. These efforts were costly and often roundly criticized for encouraging mass migration.[6]

In the economic decline that followed the Napoleonic Wars, governments financed migration as a way to export rampant poverty. In the 1820s, the British government, under the direction of Under Secretary for War and the Colonies Sir Robert Wilmot-Horton, developed and implemented policies to assist these migrants to settle and work land in Upper Canada. The basis of his policy rested on the idea that it was cheaper for the government to remove the poverty stricken from the British Isles than it was to continue to assist them with parish poor funds. Beginning in 1823 and again in 1825, the British government gave assistance to over twenty-five hundred Irish to settle in Upper

Canada in the two areas of Petersborough and Lanark County.[7] With this scheme in place, Wilmot-Horton tried to push through another initiative that would have given families on poor relief the option to exchange assisted passages, grants of colonial land, and assistance with housing, stock, and equipment for farming in return for surrendering future legal rights to parish poor relief. The financing of this program would have come from a new system of government loans directly to the parishes. This grander scheme was never implemented because Wilmot-Horton left the Colonial Office. His successors abandoned his program of government-assisted emigration, and his ideas were never implemented as he designed them.[8] By 1826, the British government turned away from assisted emigration programs as a way to relieve themselves of paupers. Instead, it endorsed the establishment of private enterprises such as the Petworth Emigration Committee, one of the largest and most successful private enterprises financed by the third Earl of Egremont and organized by the Reverend Thomas Sockett. They helped over eighteen hundred migrants from West Essex, Surrey, East Sussex, and Cambridgeshire travel to Ontario and saw them settled on lands in the 1830s.[9]

The British and German schemes were conventional in the sense that they encouraged their citizens to go to places where they were already going. But African Americans were invited to Haiti, an island nation that by its very existence challenged the international order of slavery tolerance. That is why—unlike the reaction to the German and British offers—the African American emigration was a political act.

* * *

In January 1824, a proposal to endorse a national solution to slavery reached the floor of the Ohio state legislature. The proposal called for a gradual emancipation scheme that would free slaves after the age of twenty-one. An unnamed foreign colony was a cornerstone of this plan. Eight other northern states signed on to the Ohio plan.[10] The same year, Haiti's President Jean-Pierre Boyer made a proposal of his own: he offered free passage, free land, and other incentives to black Americans who immigrated to Haiti. Whether or not Boyer was aware of the state initiatives, his offer dovetailed opportunely, in the eyes of some people, with these schemes to whiten America. I argue that Boyer's offer was a conscious effort to push the scales of debate in the U.S. toward Haitian emigration.

Boyer's offer to finance emigration to his nation won him some powerful U.S. media supporters who had become disillusioned with the African colonization project. Unlike the African adventure, Americans would not have to finance the Haitian experiment. Haitian emigration proponents argued that Africa's hour had passed and that it was time to try something new. Haiti was untried and unblemished, while African colonization had a poor track record, they argued. A politically disparate alliance of newspapers coalesced around Haiti and the Haitian emigration project and became formidable rivals of the ACS in the mid-1820s.

The main leaders on the Haitian side of the media blitz included Hezekiah Niles, Benjamin Lundy, and Loring Dewey.[11] Dewey, a Presbyterian minister and agent of the ACS in New York, possessed the least access to the public mind, as he was the only one of the three without a publication. Lundy and Niles were newspaper editors and publishers. Lundy devoted his *Genius of Universal Emancipation* to abolitionist causes and became the leading abolitionist of his day. Niles used his business-oriented *Weekly Register* to publicize and advocate for national and economic reforms. One of his biographers called him one of America's first economists.[12] All three became disaffected members of the ACS, frustrated with its failure to use the media effectively in attracting black Americans to migrate.[13] These men were, in many ways, pioneers of media spin. They determined to turn the tide of the colonization movement away from Africa and toward Haiti. The rationale for promoting emigration remained the same: these men and other advocates of emigration believed that if large numbers of free blacks went to the Caribbean nation (or other colonies), then slave owners would warm to the idea and manumit their slaves and free the United States of the stain of slavery once and for all. Hindsight has shown that the philanthropy of slave owners never reached beyond small numbers of manumitted slaves. During the 1820s, however, many American abolitionists believed that, if a relatively painless alternative could be presented, the "majority of the southern people, and even the slave-holders," would back the dismantling of the slave economy.[14] The transportation of slaves to Haiti appeared to be this relatively painless exit strategy. By using their access to the public media outlets of the time, Lundy, Niles, and numerous other editors who followed their lead, urged free blacks, reluctant ACS members, and slave owners to accept the golden opportunity of Haiti.[15]

Observing public opinion turn toward Haiti in the summer of 1824, the ACS acknowledged that problems had dogged its colony and even admitted, "We are fearful that our Colony at Messuarado will not realize all the favourable results which have been anticipated."[16] But the ACS continued to deflect calls to abandon the colony and pleaded for its constituents to remain patient. An obliviousness to the unfeasible nature of its mission was deeply rooted in the ACS.

The seed of the ACS was planted in the late eighteenth century when prominent American intellectuals such as Thomas Jefferson mulled the establishment of a separate territory or nation outside the United States for freed slaves and free blacks.[17] The reality of the racial animus that developed in St. Domingue during the Haitian Revolution challenged this idea, at least regarding the location of the territory in the Caribbean. Fear of Haiti's power and proximity was ever pervasive in the consciousness of southern slave owners such as Jefferson.[18] Nevertheless, Jefferson's concept of a colonial resolution of the slave debate lingered in the public forum. With the moderate success of Great Britain's Sierra Leone colony in West Africa in the 1790s, Americans began to contemplate establishing their own colony for African Americans. Indeed, the black ship captain Paul Cuffe explored the possibility of African Americans joining the colonial enterprise at Sierra Leone and worked toward this goal. Cuffe died in 1817, before his dream could be realized.

The idea of a black sanctuary gained currency in the 1810s when northerners and southerners alike grew concerned about a perceived increase in the black population, both free and enslaved. Although the overall proportion of enslaved and free people remained steady throughout the early nineteenth century—at about 20 percent of the population—certain cities and states witnessed a dramatic rise in the size of their black communities, generating a perception that the black population was proportionately much greater than it really was. The most dramatic growth in the North occurred in Baltimore, where the black population increased sharply, ballooning from 1,578 in 1790 to 14,683 in 1820, so that the black quotient of the total population surged to 23.0 percent from 11.7 percent in 1790.[19] New York City's black population climbed from 3,500 in 1800 to roughly 10,368 in 1820, and that increased the proportion of the population that was black from 4.4 percent to 6.8 percent.[20] In Philadelphia, the black population numbered 2,078 in 1790, then in 1800 hit 6,436 and rose to 12,110 in 1820, making the black population 10.7 percent of the total, up from 9.5 percent in 1790.[21]

Made anxious by this perceived baby boom among free blacks, Charles Fenton Mercer of Virginia and Robert Finley, a minister in New Jersey, began to advocate separately for free black Americans' removal to a colony in Africa.[22] The mutual interest of men from different states in this endeavor set the stage for the establishment of a national organization, and the American Colonization Society was founded in Washington, D.C., in January 1817.

Understanding the power of celebrity, the ACS reached out to famous people. Members included such luminaries as the famous orator and politician Henry Clay and Bushrod Washington, the nephew and symbolic heir of George Washington. The ACS attracted support from all across the United States, quickly establishing auxiliary societies in states north and south of the Mason-Dixon line.[23] Its platform called for the removal of free blacks and freed slaves and was devised to appeal to both antislavery and slave-owning Americans. As one supporter of African American removal put it, colonization promised "a time when [the United States] shall be one homogenous nation."[24] The organization's mass appeal stretched it thin, however, making decisive action elusive.

Many free blacks and antislavery whites developed deep animosity to the group, growing suspicious of the ACS's motives, especially after many members were exposed as slaveholders. For some antislavery supporters, whether the society believed in abolition or the perpetuation of slavery mattered little since "their exertions must" eventually bring about "universal emancipation," as one prominent newspaper, the *National Recorder*, put it. As for their comrade slave owners' reluctance to emancipate, antislavery ACS supporters argued that once the group had "effected a settlement—the difficulties will gradually diminish."[25] As long as the goal of black removal succeeded—and a location outside the United States was established—then the ACS's ambivalence about slavery seemed of little consequence to either of these strange bedfellows.

For some African Americans, however, the ACS's motivations proved pivotal. In an 1819 New Year's speech celebrating the end of the Atlantic slave trade, Lewis Tapsico, a "colored man," took the opportunity to castigate the ACS as a whole and warned that "a momentous crisis" had arrived for the African American community. Pointing to the "strange contradiction" that slaveholders would take an interest in promoting the happiness of free descendants of Africa, Tapsico believed it was "plain as light itself" that the true object behind African colonization was "to get rid of the free colored people." He argued that the ACS wanted to remove the idea that people of color could be free. Tapsico concluded with this indictment: "The more this plan of colonization is examined, the more disgusting and shocking do its features appear."[26] Following Tapsico's speech, a meeting was called in Philadelphia in which three thousand black Philadelphians gathered to publicly reject Africa and the ACS's plan. The meeting's attendants, led by James Forten, a wealthy black sailmaker, unanimously found that African colonization "would stay the cause of the entire abolition of slavery," something they as a community could not tolerate.[27] Forten later reported that there was not one soul who favored African colonization at the meeting.[28] Such African American opposition proved detrimental to the ACS's recruitment goals.[29]

Despite northern African Americans' public opposition, ACS members remained hopeful that a successful colony would cause the community to rally around the project and "feel more strongly the desire of a country where they may enjoy the equality which they never can attain" in the United States.[30] This desire never fully materialized. The first location of the colony, Sherbro Island, was a farce, and settlers abandoned it after a few weeks, mostly because of the site's unsuitability for human habitation. The island possessed neither fresh water nor a working harbor. The colony and its administrators relocated to a place called Cape Mesurado, in what was later called Liberia. The colonial administrators' lack of preparation and foresight was glaringly clear from this and other blunders reported to the American public. This wrong-footed beginning put off potential colonists: from 1820 to 1824, only three hundred African Americans ventured to Monrovia, the ACS's new capital at Cape Mesurado.

Cape Mesurado proved only slightly more welcoming than Sherbro Island. Settlers suffered from what the press termed "African fevers"—malaria and yellow fever. This affliction took administrators, naval officers, and settlers alike. At one point, more than forty colonists took ill simultaneously, and the death rates spiraled upward. By 1824, 85 out of the 225 colonists who had moved to Liberia had died.[31] This level of illness and death made cultivating food and developing trade relations difficult. As a result, the colony continued to depend on stores of food and trade items brought from the United States, hardly fulfilling the image of a self-sufficient satellite envisioned by the administrators. Organizers began to understand the Herculean task they had set themselves—the time, effort, money, and lives expended in establishing a colony from scratch in an unforgiving climate.

Survival alone was costly. Poor relations with neighboring indigenous peoples meant that the colony also required cannon, muskets, gun powder, and military assistance. American troops forced the Dei people to turn over the Cape Mesurado land. The settlement fended off two large-scale attacks from the displaced people. Seven of the settlers' children were kidnapped during one battle. In the subsequent months, forty more arrivals died.[32] It is small wonder that farming and trading were slow to develop when security and health issues loomed so large.

In the 1820s African colonization under the ACS was an abject failure.[33] Promoted as an idyllic self-sufficient settlement that would discourage the illegal trade of African slaves, the colony could barely protect itself. Other reports reached the United States that slavers had been spotted leaving the British colony of Sierra Leone, further undermining convictions that African colonization would end the illegal slave trade.[34] One antislavery observer wrote, "The Mesurado Colony, is, and must ever be, a feeble, and comparatively, inoperative palliative of this evil."[35] While making little headway in either establishing a black colony's independence or eradicating the illegal slave trade, the project also broke the ACS's bank.

The colony's costs ran so high, between $4,000 and $6,000 a year, that the ACS's treasury was empty by 1822. Donations, which had helped sustain it, also dried up as news of the colony's problems reached the United States. By 1823, the ACS acknowledged publicly that it "had arrived at a crisis."[36] Many members felt that without some sort of large government assistance, they would have to abandon the colony.[37] Pessimism reigned. As Lundy concluded in his newspaper the *Genius of Universal Emancipation*, the ACS had spent "immense sums," and more would be required "to effect any thing of importance, upon the plan which they have devised."[38] Niles of the *Weekly Register* warned that sending African Americans to Africa would cost "millions of dollars a year" and predicted that not even "the whole revenue of the United States" could accomplish an independent and secure colony.[39] The prognosis for the colony and the ACS looked grim.

Conscious of the public failure of the colony, members debated desperate measures to salvage it. In 1823, Leonard Bacon—the brother of Samuel Bacon, one of the colonial administrators in the initial African expedition to Sherbro Island—suggested that to "quicken" and "dramatize" colonization, the ACS must charter four ships every year to leave from the large port cities of New York, Boston, Charleston, and Providence. Even if the ships sailed half empty, merely by placing ads in various local newspapers, the ACS would give the positive impression that colonization was progressing. Bacon hoped that this "spinning" of public opinion would in fact bring about the desired result.[40] The ACS never implemented any of his proposals.

* * *

The ACS's inertia frustrated supporters, and this frustration surfaced in newspaper editorials and other publications. Even before the summer of 1824, Benjamin Lundy predicted that if the ACS continued along the same path, "disastrous occurrences" awaited its colony.[41] Hezekiah Niles seconded this doubt when he wrote that Africa had little prospect of "producing any sensible effect, as to a reduction of the amount of the black population among us."[42] He tabulated in another article, "With all of our [ACS] exertions, at a great cost of money and sacrifice of life, we have sent only about 300 persons."[43] This number, a paltry few compared to the tens of thousands originally projected by the ACS, did little to achieve the whitening of America. Niles's disillusionment with the African project was made clear both to the public and to members of the ACS when he began to advocate for Haitian emigration. He gave sustained coverage to the project: almost every edition of *Niles' Weekly Register* beginning June 24, 1824, contained at least one article on Haiti or Haitian emigration and how much better Haiti would be than Africa as a black settlement. And he joined the Baltimore Haytian Emigration Society in June 1824.[44] Niles used his publication to put pressure on the ACS and its members who had proved reluctant to embrace Haitian emigration.

Niles made some inroads on the ACS constituency in New York City. At a public meeting called to discuss the two plans, the participants declared the ACS colony Mesurado a failure and the continuation of any project involving African colonization useless. The *New York Commercial Advertiser* reported on the meeting.[45]

The press figures who backed the Haitian project were motivated by different goals. All were disillusioned members of the ACS. Haitian emigration reanimated Lundy, Niles, and Dewey, supporters of African colonization who had seen their dreams of a white America scuttled on African shores.[46] To them, Haiti was the ideal destination for a quick and efficient removal of the black population. They sold the idea of Haiti to their readership by citing favorable costs, the anticipated commercial benefits to American merchants, and the project's abolitionist credentials.

A cost-based analysis of African colonization and Haitian emigration convinced many people of the merits of Haiti over Africa. Comparing the transportation costs alone showed how much more practical Haiti was—for one person to sail to Haiti, the estimated cost was between twelve and fourteen dollars. In order to send one person to Africa, the costs doubled to twenty-six dollars. With these lowered costs, far greater numbers could be settled, it was argued. Haitian emigration would also exact far less of a long-term financial commitment. Boyer's offer included paying the settlers' passage and donations of food, supplies, and land. These offers left America with far less financial responsibility for the settlers than African colonization did.

In Haiti, established trade networks existed already and bore the potential for expansion. As the *National Advocate* remarked, American emigrants would "carry with them American particularities and feelings," ensuring "the influence of these upon the commerce of Hayti."[47] These sentiments were often repeated in American newspapers. As Niles noted, "Every one can perceive perfectly" that emigration would be "an infallible means of augmenting the commerce of the United States."[48] American emigrants with their American tastes and preferences could potentially make trade with Haiti even more profitable: once American emigrants settled in and began to prosper, they would want to buy American goods and products that they had been accustomed to in the United States. Their acquisitiveness would spur growth in both nations.

The promise of trade between the United States and Haiti also won abolitionists to the cause. Although few public pronouncements were made about Haiti's antislavery potential, abolitionists envisioned making it the centerpiece of the free produce movement, a consumer-driven campaign against the sale and use of products from slave labor.[49] In Haiti, unlike almost every place in the New World in 1824, no ambiguity existed as to whether the laborers working in the fields were free or enslaved, making Haitian products and crops ideally suited to the free produce movement.[50] With the introduction of more laborers from the United States, Haiti was in a perfect position to supply this new market.

First conceived in England as a political and consumer boycott of slave-grown sugar, the free produce movement organized as a grass-roots movement in 1791, in a campaign to abolish the Atlantic slave trade. As a result of the campaign, more than three hundred thousand Britons abstained from using sugar in protest over the use of slave labor.[51] The free produce movement in nineteenth-century America exerted economic pressure in an attempt to end slavery. Advocates of the boycott envisioned free laborers cultivating and manufacturing products that would compete directly with slave-produced goods.[52] This movement involved both producers and consumers: with the increased availability of free labor products, it was hoped that conscientious consumers would opt for goods made by free hands. If a large enough market developed for free labor products, advocates believed, the movement could eventually drive slave products—and slavery—out of existence. These goods—from coffee, tobacco, sugar, and cotton to manufactured items such as cloth and clothing—would be comparably priced and untainted by the immorality or brutality of slavery.

The free produce movement in the nineteenth century was closely aligned with Haitian emigration.[53] To Elias Hicks and Charles Collins, two prominent New York Quakers, Haiti was key to their project for defeating slavery. Elias Hicks began supporting the free produce movement as early as 1811 in *Observations on the Slavery of the Africans and Their Descendants, and on the Use of the Products of Their Labor*.[54] Hicks publicly advocated for Haitian emigration and hosted a meeting devoted to the project in his Long Island home in the summer of 1824. Hicks also corresponded with Charles Collins about emigration.[55] Collins, a grocer, stocked his Cherry Street store entirely with free produce goods from 1817 to 1843, making it the first store devoted entirely to goods produced without slave labor.[56] Collins also publicly supported Haitian emigration—he hosted Jonathas Granville at his home during the Haitian agent's stay in New York.[57] He also sold the fifty thousand pounds of Haitian coffee that Boyer sent to pay for the emigrants' transportation costs.[58]

Lundy also worked for the development of the consumer boycott.[59] He advertised Charles Collins's grocery store in *Genius* and made one of the first public pronouncements on Haiti's role in promoting the system of free labor in his December 1824 edition. Lundy also pointed out that goods purchased from Haiti could be bought "without contributing to the gains of oppression." This was, he believed, a subject that deserved "serious attention."[60] Lundy continued his work throughout the 1820s and became one of the leading voices of the free produce movement.[61]

If Haiti proved a popular alternative to Africa among free blacks, it would surely work for freed slaves, these advocates believed. As these public-opinion makers shifted support from Africa to Haiti, their efforts to recruit others can be traced in the newspaper coverage of the day. As an example of the attention Haiti garnered, at least eleven different U.S. newspapers reported on the arrival of Jonathas Granville, Boyer's representative, who had been sent to the U.S. to organize and finalize emigration plans during the summer of 1824.[62]

Conscious of the emergence of Haiti as a rival to the African project, the ACS launched a counterattack. It urged members "to take no measures on behalf of Haitian emigration."[63] Members who supported Haitian emigration faced punitive measures. The leadership committee asked one of its New York members, Loring Dewey, to resign his membership in the ACS because of his public support of Haitian emigration. Whether other defectors such as Niles and Lundy were asked to resign their membership in the ACS is unknown. Soon thereafter, the ACS initiated its own media campaign against Haiti in New York, as seen in the pages of the *New York Commercial Advertiser* throughout the summer of 1824.

In this campaign, the ACS warned that—unlike the continent of Africa—the island of Haiti was far too small for the entire black American population to settle.[64] Using the sort of pseudoscience that was eventually to become a central tenet of marketing, these editorials claimed that Haiti was not the natural habitat of African descendants as Africa was and would, therefore, be less conducive to mass settlement. Other drawbacks highlighted the fact that Haiti offered nothing as a destination to the fight against the illegal slave trade or to the twin missions of Christianizing and civilizing Africa.[65] There was an ulterior motive downplayed in these editorials. ACS spokespersons eventually conceded that Haiti's proximity to the United States was a factor in their opposition, admitting that if the ACS supported Haitian emigration, it would lose the support of slave-owning constituents whose "alarms and apprehensions" were heightened at the prospect of Haitian emigration.[66]

Haitian emigration supporters responded to the ACS's attacks by exposing their rivals' concessions to southern slave owners' fears of Haiti. They also tried to debunk the ACS's arguments. One newspaper stated that—contrary to public statements about Haiti's size—the "republic could receive all the colored persons of the United States, bond or free, at once, without being over-stocked."[67] As for the ACS's contention that Haitian emigration contributed nothing to Christianizing or abolishing slavery in Africa, Lundy scoffed at this "flimsy pretext." Clearly, he pointed out, the Cape Mesurado project also showed scant progress on these fronts. If the ACS wished to do away with slavery as it avowed, Lundy asked, "why not choose a place where we have the means of sending a sufficient number"?[68]

Engaging with southerners' fears and turning the ACS's alarmism about Haiti around, a writer in the *National Gazette* argued that plantation owners should support Haitian emigration for their own security. This might be termed the safety-valve argument. The deportation of radical blacks could downgrade a domestic crisis to a foreign-policy issue.[69] Other supporters of the Haitian approach, such as Niles, tried to persuade critics that accepting Haitian emigration was pragmatic for both national-security and economic reasons. For those who feared that cooperating with Haiti on the issue would be akin to nursing a viper at the U.S. bosom, Niles wrote, "our object should be to cultivate the best disposition in the people of Hayti" by accepting and encouraging emigration.[70] To Niles, establishing friendly relations with Haiti would ultimately help the southern United States by improving trade and providing a place for the removal of black Americans. He pointed to practical rather than ideological grounds for backing

Haitian emigration: "It is an event that must be expected—one that we cannot prevent."[71]

In the northern United States, Haiti had become a cause célèbre by 1824. Newspapers heralded the departure dates of ships, sometimes weeks in advance. Indeed, newspaper publishers and editors such as Niles, Lundy, and Robert Walsh were instrumental in marketing Haiti to the public. They published minutes of meetings, Haitian emissary Granville's speeches, emigration-office addresses, and eventually letters written by emigrants. They promoted the Haitian emigration project to a wide readership.

To supporters of Haitian emigration, the thousands of free black Americans who signed up to sail for Haiti—in contrast to the more tepid response to African colonization—were the proof of the pudding. In October 1824, the editor of *Poulson's American Daily Advertiser* pointed out that "vessel after vessel is dispatched" and confidently concluded, "emigration to Hayti is progressing with unexampled rapidity; it is not a mere experiment."[72] Another newspaper estimated that from Philadelphia alone, "18 vessels have sailed or about sailing from Philadelphia, which will carry about 2,000 emigrants."[73] These numbers appeared to support the position of Lundy and his cohorts—that emigration to Haiti would whiten America in far less time and for far less money than African colonization would. As Lundy boasted, "I should be pleased to see a statement of the expenses already incurred, in planting the colony of *three hundred persons* at Monrovia, within the last six years, that I might contrast it with the amount of cost in transporting the five thousand, to Hayti, in a period of six *months*."[74] Lundy believed that the United States had finally found a "judicious system" for the "riddance of our country of its black population."[75] For Lundy and other white believers, these departures justified the heated public battle waged against African colonization and gave them hope that Haiti could save America from slavery and the racial discord they feared. They also expected—as did Boyer—that formal diplomatic relations, even recognition, would be established once Haitian emigration proved itself. Learning from the shortcomings in the ACS's publicity campaign, proponents of Haitian emigration made use of newspapers in advancing their project. What remained to be seen was whether these claims of superiority for Haiti as a destination would be borne out in the experiences of the emigrants.

The ACS was not persuaded, however, and stuck to its goal of African colonization. Perhaps bowing to Haiti's popularity in the Northeast, the ACS ceased fund-raising in New York and Pennsylvania in the 1820s. Still, it reorganized and refocused at the national level.[76] The ACS leadership also adopted the tactics of their rivals and published the first edition of its own organ, the *African Repository and Colonial Journal*, in the winter of 1825.[77] The ACS may have been waiting for the negative publicity that would follow the utopic descriptions about life in Haiti. As they well knew, life in a new place was often far harder than expected.

The other migrations from the time period also attest to this. Those Germans who followed Gottfried Duden to the U.S. learned firsthand that the travel writer's experience was far from typical, and they were caught unawares by the strenuous existence that made up life for most people in early nineteenth-century Missouri. Duden had hired his neighbor to do much of the day-to-day farming and employed a German housekeeper to do almost everything else. There was such a public outcry from Germans who followed Duden's advice and settled in Missouri that Duden was compelled to respond. He tried to remedy the boosterish tone of his report by writing a second book, called *Self-Accusation Concerning His Travel Report, to Warn against Further Rash Emigration* (1834). Although the book was framed as a corrective, Duden attempted to shift the blame on the "common herd" who read his letters of advice without heeding or understanding them.[78] Despite Duden's efforts to discourage mass migration, thousands continued to flock to Missouri, many with his books in hand. By 1860, more than thirty-eight thousand German speakers settled in the "Show Me State."

Wilmot-Horton and his Irish emigration scheme to Upper Canada also experienced negative media about the settlement process. The project brought two groups of Irish residents; the first group consisted of 568 Cork residents, mostly unemployed artisans and farmers, and the second, about two thousand Irish from the Munster counties of Cork, Kerry, and Limerick. All took up the government's offer of free land and provisions and housing if they paid their own way. The scheme was extremely popular among the Irish, allowing Wilmot-Horton to select families and individuals from applicants. Upon their arrival, however, many were rumored to have abandoned the lands and migrated to the United States at the first available opportunity. This proved detrimental to the public image of the project. Even when commentators and on-the-ground witnesses reported that these rumors were unfounded and the migrants themselves expressed their appreciation and gratitude in letters and reports, the predominant narrative of the project as a failure was difficult to derail.[79] The project also overran the initial estimate of twelve pound sterling per family provided by Wilmot-Horton. The hostility and even violence with which these Irish migrants were welcomed by their British Protestant neighbors was the last straw. There was little that Wilmot-Horton or his supporters could do to combat the negative image.[80] The high cost, the persistent rumors of ungrateful migrants, and the discord that the migration provoked could not be overcome, and the British government turned away from publicly funded migration projects for more than half a century.

Perhaps learning from the apparent failure to control the public image of the Wilmot-Horton migration, the organizers and funders of the Petworth Emigration Committee, which operated during the 1830s, maintained tight control over the public image presented of the migrants and the migration process. The efforts of Rev. Thomas Sockett, the organizer of the Petworth scheme, harnessed the power of the emigrant letters to promote the migration. He collected and printed migrant letters to help keep interest in the emigration strong. He understood that direct marketing worked, and when one of the ships leaving for Canada lacked the requisite number of emigrants, he quickly organized a new printout of letters for public consumption. His publications gave such a good impression of Canada that land companies used his books of emigrant letters to sell and promote the purchase of Canadian lands.[81] Historians who have studied these letters and the mediation of Sockett as editor have concluded that his selection of letters to be printed depended on his judgment of the letter writer and whether he or she fit his idea of a "solid emigrant" with "good prospects." Many of the letter writers had deep roots in their English communities and would have been well-known by their contemporaries, thus helping to promote the project even more.[82] Although some readers of these letters voiced distrust of these publications, Sockett and his printer answered these concerns with public assurances that the original letters were available and could be read and examined for omissions.[83] Sockett even described his editing process in his books, assuring his audience that "the very *words* of the writers" were used, even when misspellings and repetition occurred.[84]

His control of the public face of the Petworth project and the way he spun the letters are vital to British historians' understanding of the emigration.[85] Those who wanted to control the public view of Haitian emigration faced a far-tougher task, as both supporters and opponents understood the power of emigrant testimony. Even today, the "success" of the Haitian emigration project is contested.

* * *

When Boyer advertised Haiti as an emigrant destination for free and enslaved African Americans in 1824, he was capitalizing on the positive media attention that Haiti had received in American newspapers. Boyer's proposal was embraced by his U.S. allies as an expedient answer to the U.S. race question. Others worried that the offer came with hidden strings. Skeptics predicted that Boyer would demand American recognition of Haiti in exchange for opening up his country.[86] This was, of course, not far from the truth. As shown in chapter 3, many of the newspaper editors who supported emigration were also public advocates for American recognition of Haiti. Like Boyer, Niles, Lundy, Dewey, and others were anxious to improve Haitian-American relations, a miscegenation that the ACS's slave-owning membership would never countenance. The ACS could do little but watch and wait as shipload after shipload of African American passengers sailed to Haiti's shores seeking a new life.

5 / Push and Pull in Haitian Emigration

In 1824 and 1825, a range of social pressures pushed African American individuals to leave everything they knew in America, and a variety of hopes pulled them to settle in Haiti. Each migration was a mixture of push and pull factors, and each was motivated as much by the America left behind as by the hoped-for Haiti.[1] Backgrounds varied widely. The travelers included families, single men, and even single women. They came from all social levels—laundresses and merchants, skilled artisans and unskilled day laborers, farmers and urbanites. Such prominent figures as John Allen, son of Rev. Bishop Richard Allen; Dr. Belfast Burton of Philadelphia; John Sommersett, a cigar maker and church leader of the Philadelphia AME Bethel Church; and a former Presbyterian minister, Benjamin F. Hughes, all chose to move to Haiti. Other individuals, whose stories and motivations are only reaching posterity for the first time, include Abel Reed, an educated young New York African American; a ship carpenter named King from Baltimore; Hannah Quincy, a New York laundress; William Baldwin, another New Yorker, with his wife and two children, Serena and William Jr.; and the farming family the Butlers from the Mid-Atlantic state of Pennsylvania or Maryland, traveling eleven strong: the patriarch Charles Butler, his wife, and nine children with ages ranging from eleven to twenty. These individuals and their stories are representative case studies of this emigration and the promises, expectations, and fears that motivated it.

Each narrative shares some elements: a sense of alienation from mainstream American life, a belief in the potential for financial or other advancement in Haiti, and a desire to be united as a people in a black nation.[2] All sought to work for the betterment of themselves, for Haiti, and for their brethren in chains. Pushed out of an America that refused to treat them as equals, these Americans saw in Haiti a place where the political and economic opportunities that were closed to them in their native country were readily available. They were all drawn to a country that offered a republican government where they could vote without prejudice of color or property and where the skin color that increasingly set them apart as outcasts in the U.S was privileged. Haiti was in every way presented and understood to be their black "land of the free."

* * *

By the 1820s, the black inhabitants of Philadelphia, Baltimore, and New York lived in well-established communities that were served by black-run schools, churches, and institutions. Some were dispersed through neighborhoods; others clustered together on certain streets.[3] Many were sizeable. Baltimore contained the largest black population, with over fourteen thousand free blacks and another ten thousand slaves. Philadelphia and New York City both housed more than twelve thousand free blacks and very small slave populations. For northern African Americans, city life was increasingly the norm—in stark contrast to the rest of the United States, where less than 4 percent of the population lived in urban communities.[4] Not all the Haitian emigrants were urban residents, however; many farmers also chose to relocate to Haiti.

In 1820, life in the United States was becoming increasingly difficult for free African Americans (and for many poor white Americans) as the country stagnated in a deep and prolonged recession sparked by the Panic of 1819, the worst financial crisis to hit the young republic. Specific numbers are unavailable for African American joblessness, but in Philadelphia alone, between 1816 and 1819, almost seven thousand workers were laid off.[5] In 1820, the New York Society for the Prevention of Pauperism estimated that twelve thousand people—10 percent of the city's population—sought poor relief.[6]

The economic downturn most deeply affected African American workers because they were among the most vulnerable population—the working poor. While the average laborer in the United States could expect one dollar a day, African Americans, who often worked as unskilled laborers in the Northeast, earned much less. Compounding the difficulties for African Americans living in New York and Philadelphia was the arrival of Irish and German immigrants.[7] These new arrivals crowded the streets with cheap labor and drove up the costs of housing. The Panic also hit the agricultural sector. Farmers, who had seen unprecedented prices for their crops during the Napoleonic Wars, saw economic ruin when the Panic hit, causing prices on flour, rice, and cotton to fall between 35 and 50 percent. And whether working as domestics, farmhands, maritime laborers, or elsewhere, unskilled workers experienced declining wages.[8]

Not all African Americans worked as unskilled laborers, however. Some found positions as semiskilled and skilled laborers such as cloth makers, spinsters, shoemakers, and tailors. For these artisans, the Panic only added to the economic woes that had started for them after the ending of the Napoleonic Wars with the unleashing of pent-up British manufacturing capacities on the American market. During the war, goods that had been languishing in warehouses in Great Britain were dusted off and shipped en masse to the American market. Structural changes within the workplace also added to the declining fortunes of the artisan class. With the introduction of manufacturing, the traditional craft system that masters, journeymen, and apprentices had participated in for centuries lost its grip. Skills that had once required years of training were now activities that any laborer could perform on the first day of the job. During the 1820s, these two labor systems, the traditional craft shop and the large capitalized factories, overlapped.[9] And just as jobs moved to factories, African Americans faced exclusion from this new labor system as whites refused to work alongside them in the close quarters required.[10] Among these African Americans, moving to Haiti provided opportunities to open their own shops and work their own trades, a throwback to better times in a world transformed. For others, who accepted that the traditional craft system was irrevocably lost and envisioned becoming entrepreneurs, Haiti also beckoned.

Charlotte Erickson, one of the premier historians of English emigration, detected broad distinctions between emigrants who settled within the British Empire and those who settled in the United States after independence. Those who migrated to Canada often did so for professional reasons, while those who went to the United States typically sought adventure and a new life.[11] The limited choices for African American emigrants meant that Haiti represented both economic opportunity and a sense of rebirth. The most instructive comparison in English emigration history is likely the early Puritan settlers. They were pushed out of England for both economic and socioreligious reasons. They were drawn to the New World by tales of opportunity but also viewed it as a last resort. Similar social, political, and economic dynamics pushed and pulled individuals to accept Boyer's offer to settle in Haiti.

This economic pressure came just as African Americans faced political constraints with the passage of suffrage laws that limited black voting. In New York, the African American community retained the right to vote but needed substantial property to qualify. Property requirements for white males, in contrast, had been suspended, allowing all adult white males to participate regardless of their property qualifications. In other states, political color bars were well established. In Maryland, free blacks had been prohibited from voting since 1810. Even in Pennsylvania—the cradle of liberty—laws restricting free black rights routinely came under review in the state legislature. These laws proposed preventing free blacks from traveling into the state; they also moved to require all free blacks to register and obtain freedom certificates. And if free African Americans were convicted of a crime, they were to be sold into slavery and their purchase price given to their victims as "compensation."[12] Although these proposals never passed into law, each time the state considered such actions, the African American community felt the sting of racial persecution acutely, and the cumulative effect was a chronic threat of greater oppression. Many blacks recognized how diminished their prospects were for prosperity, equality, or liberty in early 1820s America.

These feelings of constraint were echoed in the towns and farms throughout Ireland and German-speaking areas of central Europe in the 1810s and 1820s. According to officials of the time who reported on German migration, "the Auswanderung mania" came from a "certain despair of the possibility of a future in the Fatherland."[13] Another observer, Frederick List, noted to the Wurttemberg government that "a deep discontent, that is, oppression, lack of freedom," as well as "excessive taxes and dues, and the suppression of all sorts of civil rights" pushed people out to America.[14]

Irish Catholics had seen the suppression of their civil rights since the late seventeenth century, when the Penal Laws were first enacted. Beginning in 1695, the British Crown, in retaliation for the Irish Catholic support of Catholic Stuart King James II and his bid for the throne, passed a series of laws that have come to be called the Penal Laws. These laws prevented Irish Catholics from military participation in the Royal Navy or British Army, work that gave steady income and provided upward mobility for many. Irish Catholics were prevented from voting, holding political office, bearing arms, or practicing their religion, as Catholicism was outlawed. In addition to banning their religion, the Irish language, Gaelic Irish, was forbidden. Landed property was made deliberately smaller by a government system that required partible inheritance for practicing Irish Catholics; thus, all the land had to be divided equally among male heirs. This system created smaller and smaller fields, which diluted the value and productivity of the land. If one of the heirs declared himself a Protestant, he inherited the entire estate. The system succeeded, and by the end of the eighteenth century, Irish Protestants owned 95 percent of the land on the island. As one observer noted upon visiting the island in 1835, Ireland "was an entire nation of paupers."[15]

In the U.S., because work was scarce during this economic restructuring and white exclusion was becoming ever more prevalent in daily life, African Americans responded to Boyer's carefully tailored proposal to settle in Haiti. Although he advertised to all classes of African Americans, Boyer was most pressed to find farmers and laborers. American laborers would revive the plantation economy of Haiti, while the artisans and professionals would bring skills and capital that the nation needed. These skills would stimulate the economy by increasing the export capacity of Haiti and by developing and strengthening the nascent manufacturing sector.[16] Because Haiti's economy was so heavily geared toward export crops, Boyer's master plan for the bulk of the emigrants was to use them as farmers and laborers in strengthening the coffee and sugar trade, which had been the basis of St. Domingue's enormous wealth and prosperity.

To meet the labor demands of the island, Boyer essentially proposed three separate plans for African Americans: one for farmers, another for sharecroppers and laborers, and a third for artisans and professionals. Farmers would receive three acres of land per person. Black farmers who had struggled to obtain title to good land in the United States were promised freehold grants of three acres per person upon moving to Haiti. A family of five could start with a fifteen-acre farm before having to purchase any land. While those who sharecropped land would receive valuable experience cultivating crops and after one or two years, they, too, would be eligible for land. Nor would they have to go to the expense of buying farming tools. Mechanics and professionals received exemptions on taxes for one year, enabling them to establish businesses without any additional expenses. All the American settlers could expect four months of food provisions and their passage to Haiti on chartered vessels.[17] Of course, Boyer's offer was a rare chance of relief in such hard times. Among the British Isles migrations between 1815 and 1845, only 10 percent of those who migrated (this 10 percent includes the Petworth and the Wilmot-Horton groups discussed in chapter 4) received financial assistance from the state, the parish, or a philanthropic organization. This number is a far cry from the Boyer plan, in which close to 100 percent of those who migrated traveled with assistance. Among the German-speaking Europeans who emigrated, there was almost no financial assistance available.[18]

For William Baldwin and his wife and children—Serena, age twelve; and William, age ten—migrating to Haiti was an act of hope and a significant risk. In 1824, the family lived in the "Five Points" section of New York, on Orange Street—one of the three streets that crossed to create the infamous intersection. Five Points in the 1820s, however, had not yet become the den of vice and crime that would make it notorious. Baldwin, who in the 1819 Jury List possessed $150 worth of property, was not wealthy by New York standards. For an African American, however, he was well-off and possessed enough disposable income that the family lived alone, an uncommon luxury among the city's African American community, whose householders often supplemented their incomes by taking in boarders.[19] And rather than send Serena out to service, the family chose to—and had the means to—educate their only daughter at the African Free School.[20]

What allowed for the Baldwins' relative comfort was William's job as an oysterman.[21] That job description encompassed everything from selling shucked oysters on street corners to running an entertainment establishment such as that operated by Thomas Downing, one of the most successful New York African Americans, who was also known as an "oysterman."[22] Where Baldwin's oystering business fell in this range remains unknown. Posterity does suggest that neither adult Baldwin could read or write, since Serena, rather than her parents, penned letters back to the United States.[23] Because of William's work along the waterfront, he could have known other languages, such as Spanish, Dutch, and French, through daily contact with the thousands of international visitors to his city. New York City's participation in international trade, even in the early part of the nineteenth century, made it one of the most cosmopolitan cities in the United States. As one commentator noted in the 1830s, German, French, Spanish, and Italian could all be heard on Broadway.[24] Baldwin possibly traveled to Haiti earlier as a sailor, since 40 percent of free African American men in the North shipped out at some point in their lives.[25] The Baldwins departed from New York sometime in September, but precisely when remains unknown. On arrival on the Caribbean island, the family settled in the new Haitian territory of Santo Domingo, where Spanish continued to be the primary language. Perhaps William knew Spanish better than French, but we do not know.

Despite the relative comfort of the Baldwins' New York City life, William had good reason to be disenchanted. As a property holder who could lawfully exercise his voting privileges before 1821, Baldwin certainly would have chafed at the new 1821 New York State Constitution, which imposed onerous property qualifications on African Americans—a flagrantly inequitable law. In Haiti, no such constraints on political participation existed. And William probably looked at his son and namesake as well as his daughter and realized how limited their futures were in such an unequal society.

Like many African Americans, Baldwin may have learned about the emigration project directly from Haytian Emigration Society meetings. These meetings provided opportunities to speak personally to Jonathas Granville, the Haitian representative of the emigration project, who was touring African American communities on behalf of Boyer. Although it is difficult to measure the influence of these meetings in persuading those who hesitated to leave the United States, Granville's speeches open a window into the content of the meetings. In one extant speech, Granville described the bleak prospects for those who remained in the United States and said that more than their own future was at stake—they must think of their children, "those precious objects of your solicitude," because Haiti, he said, "will awaken them, not to a deeper sense of evils they must endure, and the degradations they must suffer" but to a fuller "sense of the blessings of Providence."[26] These sentiments surely resonated with the audience, as Granville addressed the dreams of all parents throughout history—that their children enjoy better lives and opportunities than they experienced.

But for Baldwin, and all those with children, settling in Haiti involved risk, as rumors on both sides of the Atlantic circulated of a possible French attack.[27] Because of these rumors, Granville spent time reassuring audience members that Boyer had the French situation under control.[28] Haiti's troubles with its former colonial ruler, France, continued into the 1820s and had even intensified. In the spring of 1822, a French squadron invaded the town of Samana in the former Santo Domingo, taking hostages and killing Haitian soldiers.[29] Then a small insurrection took place in Martinique that some observers in France blamed on Haitian instigators.[30] At the same time, French men-of-war battleships were reported to be assembling in Martinique, fueling rumors of a possible all-out assault by the French on the entire island.[31]

In addition to these events, Boyer's efforts to negotiate French recognition failed spectacularly. Not only did France refuse to recognize Haiti's independence, but France demanded that Haiti yield its hard-fought sovereignty and become a French tributary.[32] Fearing the worst, Boyer readied the port cities, and French merchants left the island.[33] Despite this situation, some families with children, such as the Baldwins, decided that the benefits of life in Haiti outweighed these imminent dangers.

For a Baltimore ship carpenter by the name of King, the dangers present in Haiti were offset by the economic enticements and job security offered. Baltimore in the 1820s had become one of the top-three ports for shipbuilding in the United States, largely because of skilled black shipbuilders and caulkers. And though shipbuilding remained an occupation open to African Americans in the 1820s, here, too, whites increasingly elbowed them out. Carpentry, the most highly paid work in a ship yard, was almost exclusively the preserve of whites.[34] Frederick Douglass, who worked as a slave caulker at Fells Point in Gardener's shipyard, experienced first-hand how strongly white carpenters resented "having their labor brought into competition with that of a colored freeman" and had seen how these white carpenters had repeatedly attempted to drive "the black freeman out of the ship-yard."[35] If the white carpenters' efforts to keep the shipyard white were as violent as what Douglass himself experienced, King and other black carpenters feared for their very lives. In one incident, Douglass's face "was beaten and battered most horribly" when four fellow apprentices attacked him. He also had to defend himself against other murderous white assaults and grew so fearful of the workplace that he ran away from the shipyard.[36] For black mechanics trained as ship carpenters—a highly specialized and skilled job—this treatment and color preference would have been galling.

Pushed by this sort of intimidation at the workplace, King sailed in one of the ships for Haiti—which one is unknown—in search of a place where his skills and color were in demand. Envisioning Samana as the national shipyard for Haiti, Boyer sought African Americans experienced in shipbuilding to fill its ranks and specifically requested his agent Granville to find skilled carpenters, wood sawyers, blacksmiths, caulkers, rope makers, and sailmakers.[37] Granville reportedly recruited many Philadelphian workers, including sailmakers John Newport, John Cromwell, and Moses Anderson, as well as Francis Mitchell, a shipwright.[38] In Philadelphia, shipbuilding had slowed due to competition from Boston, Baltimore, and New York shipbuilders. Of course, the economic downturn brought on by the increased competition with British traders also hurt the trade. In 1816 and 1817, the city's shipyards produced only one ship. And though the industry improved slowly in the 1820s, the city dropped to fourth place behind Boston, New York, and Baltimore in 1826.[39] As demonstrated by King's presence in Samana, Granville attracted skilled Baltimore craftsmen to the Haitian shipyards.[40]

King and the craftsmen from Philadelphia may also have considered shipbuilding as crucial to Haiti's continued independence and may have known that Samana was the target of a French attack only one year previously. A French invasion of Haiti would not just have been a battle between nations over trading rights, territory, or diplomatic issues. France had both publicly and privately vowed to reenslave the island and to reimpose the plantation system that had brought such wealth in colonial days. With this in mind, King likely was among the group of three hundred Baltimore men who traveled to Haiti without their families. Such men reportedly went to Haiti to become "Colonels and Generals" in the Haitian military, to help "wield the destinies of the nation."[41] His destination, Samana, suggests that he was not avoiding battle against the French.

Some American observers believed that the inexorable slide toward war with France enhanced the island's attractiveness to potential emigrants. African Americans, they argued, gloried "in an opportunity . . . to be placed upon the bulwark that stood between Gallic oppression & Haytien liberty."[42] As one emigrant assured his American reader in a letter, France would never succeed in conquering the island because there were "too many brave men here . . . determined to die" to defend the young nation.[43] Others claimed, "While we have no fear that Hayti will be invaded by the French, we yet would say that were it so, it should not deter our going . . . but be a motive to urge our departure."[44] Pulled by dreams of glory and by an hour of need, these Americans envisioned their military achievements in Haiti as essential to saving the island nation.[45]

Military achievements and glory may have helped pull another single male emigrant to settle in Haiti, a twenty-five-year-old by the name of Abel Reed. But the lack of opportunities in America for someone of his color, skills, and education certainly would have pushed him. Unfortunately, what work Reed pursued in America or in Haiti is unknown. He was literate, as his letters home to America indicate.[46] He might very well have been a freed slave who took his skill and advertised it in his name, someone who was "Able to Read."[47] Reed represents the many African Americans who gained an education in the United States in schools such as the African Free School in New York but continued to see the doors of opportunity closed. Frustrated by the prospects before him, Reed apparently chose to seek his fortune and use his education elsewhere. For people like Reed, the Haitian government offered clerical positions for a salary of $300 a year.[48]

Reed and others like him may have conceived of government jobs in the context of the United States' emerging spoils system. Although it did not develop into a full political tool for a few more decades, the spoils system gave political loyalists jobs in the expanding postal service and other federally funded agencies or offices. Since Jefferson's presidency, meeting the president in the White House for New Year's Day and the Fourth of July was a right conferred on ordinary Americans.[49] Jefferson even opened up the White House to the public for free tours. By the 1820s, ambitious and upwardly mobile Americans hoped to meet the president of the United States and tap him directly for civil service or military positions. Black Americans were not, however, included in this "democratization" of American politics and society. They may have hoped for similar practices in Haiti's republican system and expected Boyer to award such positions to them.[50]

Women also participated actively in the emigration to Haiti.[51] New York emigrant Hannah Quincy worked as a laundress and was apparently single.[52] As many as 60 percent of the African American women in New York probably worked as laundresses, as it was the most common work available to them.[53] Without a husband or children to keep her in the country, she would likely welcome a change from doing laundry as her sole occupation. A ticket to Haiti was Quincy's ticket out of the laundry.

Laundry in the nineteenth century was one of the most exhausting, time-consuming jobs available to a man or a woman. Lye soap was the main washing agent, and it made a scrubber's hands raw and red from use. Washing clothes for a living required maintaining boiling pots of clothes on fires, lifting tubs of water, and carrying bundles of wet clothes to the clothesline. The work did not end there. Once the clothes were dry, Hannah Quincy would have ironed the clothes with heavy hot irons. For a laundress, this was work she did every day—not just one day a week.

Women in Quincy's position were recruited to leave for Haiti by white activists. Black females were considered to be on the front lines in efforts to whiten the United States and to remove slavery. Because women bear future generations, they have an "effect on the future as well as the present population of the country," wrote one advocate for recruiting women.[54] Attracting women to leave the United States was essential to this increasingly coordinated effort. Hezekiah Niles proposed that a dowry be given to single women to find husbands in Haiti and that the money the Haytian Emigration Society collected be spent on this proposal "exclusively."[55] In this way, he hoped to encourage the settlement of women who would become mothers to Haiti's rising generation rather than to a rising generation of free black Americans.[56] Whether his suggestion was acted on remains unknown.

In New York City, unlike in Baltimore or Philadelphia, free black women outnumbered free black men two to one, leaving many unwed and supporting themselves. For black women in New York who wished to be married, the gender ratio in the city precluded many from joining in matrimony.[57] Niles predicted that these women could marry up if they left for Haiti, becoming "respected matrons." And rather than their having "vagabonds" for husbands, which would be their fate if they remained in America, he promised they would become the wives of "grave and revered senators, . . . gallant captains, independent land-holders or thrifty merchants."[58] Whether Quincy migrated to Haiti specifically for such reasons is not clear, as her marital status was not noted on the Passenger Lists. The efforts to push women out in particular suggests that people like Niles had an ulterior motive of reducing the black population in the U.S. Traditionally, advertisements for emigration had sought to attract men rather than women because men in nineteenth-century America and throughout the Atlantic world were heads of households and women were legal dependents. Wives, mothers, and daughters had little choice in the matter of immigration and were expected to follow the wishes of their menfolk. British females involved in transatlantic migrations sometimes expressed reluctance to leave their homes, as a woman named Fanny Hutton did when her husband decided to emigrate to either Canada or the United States.[59] Fanny finally joined him in Canada, but it was a touch-and-go situation until she boarded the ship. Although no evidence exists of African American women balking at the move to Haiti, it is certainly possible that many were reluctant to go to a foreign land with a different language and climate.

Boyer's language in his advertisements and publications never addressed potential female migrants. Although Boyer certainly welcomed these women, he made his promises to men. He made assurances that they would be treated as "brothers" in Haiti, and emigrants attested to this, describing in letters how they were "received more like brothers than strangers."[60] These feelings of fraternal heritage were widely held. One Haitian publication explained that African Americans and Haitians were united through the shared "blood of the *Great Africa*."[61] Framing emigration as uniting the family of Africa would certainly have appealed to African Americans such as Charles Fisher who identified themselves as African.[62]

Unfortunately, little is known about Charles Fisher's life before he settled in Haiti. In his letters to his father, who continued to live in Baltimore, Fisher said he believed the island was an "African nation" and urged "African brothers and sisters" to join him in aiding and "supporting an African government." His inclusion of women as "sisters" was a rare instance of acknowledging women's participation in the migration. In such statements, Fisher demonstrated that this shared diasporic identity had been important in his decision to move, and he articulated a version of the exhortations common to later black-nationalist movements.[63] Fisher, however, was not a blind idealist. As an American who may have only spoken English, he chose to settle in Cape Haitian, the former capital of Christophe's kingdom where the king had supported the study and use of English among his subjects.

A similar mix of antislavery ideas and practical business savvy motivated John Allen, Rev. Bishop Richard Allen's son, to move to Haiti. A tailor by trade, John Allen experienced the disruption caused by the changing business practices in the clothing industry in the 1820s. With the introduction of ready-made clothing in the 1810s and early 1820s to the United States, the traditional role of tailoring was revolutionized by the use of the "putting out" system, in which women sewed clothing pieces in their homes. This type of business model produced ready-made clothing at a fraction of the cost of tailor-made clothing.[64] Clearly, this was a push factor for a tailor. When the opportunity to migrate to Haiti came up, John Allen recognized that he was in a unique position to take his skills as a tailor to a place where they were still marketable.

John Allen's skills as a tailor would have allowed him to market and produce items for the free produce movement. Within Philadelphia's black community, support for the movement centered on Allen's father, Richard Allen, the leader of the African Methodist Episcopal Church in the United States.[65] Richard Allen joined the Free Produce Society in the 1820s and urged other African Americans to boycott slave-produced items.[66] He also contributed to the manufacture of free labor products by recruiting local black seamstresses to design bonnets and dresses to be worn and sold as symbols of abolitionist sentiment.[67] He and his son likely envisioned extending these activities in Haiti, as evidence suggests that Richard Allen and the rest of the Allen family planned to join John in Haiti. In John's October 24, 1824, letter to his father, he wrote, "I am expecting to see you here before long."[68] In the same letter, John spoke about his brother Richard's anticipated arrival date. The Allens may have anticipated a whole new line of ready-made clothing that could thrive as free labor products from the Caribbean island.[69] With an ample supply of cotton, which grew both in the wild and in cultivation in Haiti, these items would compete with the finest from the United States and Great Britain.

The free produce movement opened up many new opportunities, and Haiti appeared at the right place at the right time to participate and strengthen it. Since its earliest days as a colony, French planters in St. Domingue had produced more than eleven million pounds of cotton a year. This was a considerable amount given that most St. Domingue planters concentrated their labor and land on sugar and coffee.[70] Haitian cotton, also called "French" or "small-seed" cotton, was a very productive type of long-staple cotton that yielded three to four hundred pounds per acre and grew rapidly with two crops in a year. The island's reputation as the most profitable and productive colony in the world in the late eighteenth century continued to influence projections of Haiti's economic and agricultural potential. For those who doubted Haiti's competitive capacity, they only had to look at the island's productivity during colonial days as evidence. If the same focus of energy, manpower, and capital that once caused the sugar boom were harnessed for the growing of cotton, then Haiti could compete against the American cotton growers. Or so supporters of the free produce movement believed.[71]

Unfortunately, scant evidence of Boyer's support for free produce movement survives. Public discussions of the idea received coverage in the Haitian publication *Le Propagateur*. Although brief, the article argued that the only way the system of slavery would "quickly disappear" was for "buyers of cotton and sugar" to "exclusively" seek out items created by free labor.[72] It is possible that Boyer reduced patent duties for those who bought and sold goods for the free produce movement, as he had for the distressed merchants burned out in 1822.

In order to manufacture free labor products such as cotton cloth and clothing, the movement needed skilled laborers. John Allen, because of his father's prominent position in the African American community, had the access and the organizational power to recruit skilled artisans. A number of seamstresses, spinsters, and milliners left the reverend's dioceses in Philadelphia and New York to settle in Haiti.

Another American settler, William Edmonds from New York City, may have moved to Haiti to contribute to the free produce movement. As a retailer of tobacco, a recession-proof staple, Edmonds felt little disruption to his business caused by the Panic of 1819. Buying and selling tobacco, however, would have caused Edmonds to be directly involved with slavery and slave-produced products. Although not much is known about the tobacco business in New York City during the early decades of the nineteenth century, the tobacco sold there likely originated in the fields of Virginia or Maryland.[73] A tobacco industry existed already in Haiti, with more than 718,679 pounds of tobacco leaf exported in 1824 and more than 390,000 cigars exported in 1823, allowing Edmonds to step into an established trade.[74] Perhaps he expected to use his experience and knowledge of tobacco tastes in America to expand on the Haitian trade with the United States. In doing so, he could contribute to the destruction of slavery by supplying tobacco products that directly competed with slave-grown tobacco.[75]

Charles Butler may have sought to assist the free produce movement while turning a profit. A farmer from Pennsylvania, Butler represents migrants who sought something that was to be long denied African Americans at home—land. Fear among farmers that another financial panic would strike, wiping away their livelihood, was rife. Much of the recent scholarship on northern free blacks has emphasized how they migrated to urban environments after manumission to seek out work and fellowship.[76] While many certainly did so, some remained in rural settings and continued to work as laborers or leased land for farming.[77] Butler, an experienced farmer who had likely grown potatoes, corn, and wheat on farms in the Brandywine country, probably did not own the land he worked, because farm land was expensive in the vicinities of Philadelphia and Baltimore. Around Baltimore, for example, cultivated land without a barn or house could sell for $140 an acre, while land with an attached house and barn sold for $200 an acre.[78] In Philadelphia, land was less expensive but still quite dear: on average, a cultivated acre sold for $50.[79] As a result, it is doubtful that Butler owned his own farm.

Boyer offered African Americans land, but this was not just any land. This land, unlike in the freeholdings on offer in the western U.S. and Canada, was cleared. Cleared land eliminated the time-consuming and backbreaking weed whacking and tree cutting required with virgin land. The land could be cultivated instantly, making it immediately productive and revenue generating. Because Boyer promised three acres of land to farmers who formed a group of a dozen individuals and because Butler, his wife, and ten children made up a group of twelve, they received the full allotment of thirty-six acres. When Butler learned of what Boyer's offer would include, Haiti must have seemed a land of milk and honey.[80]

Newspapers used their columns to promote and advertise the fertility of Haiti's land. These descriptions cast Haiti as an Eden-like place, a place where settlers could see immense profits from easily harvested commodities. In one report, a writer compared the fertility of the U.S. and Haiti, concluding that the land in Haiti was three times as productive—an incredible fecundity. He wrote, "Three acres here [in Haiti]" would be as "valuable as 15 or 20 are in America, north of the Potomac."[81] These claims were another method of pitching Haiti to the African American community, and they outweighed all other discussions of what Haiti offered to the settlers. After all, land ownership was still the economic indicator of wealth in this era, and focusing on this aspect of migration to attract African Americans made perfect sense to those who wanted the project to be a success.

As for the Butlers' plot of land, if such estimates proved accurate, it would produce as much as 144 acres in America—a sizeable property.[82] Settlers themselves added to this image, as seen with an American living in Haiti who claimed he would refuse an offer of $3,000 for his Haitian land.[83] As one newspaper put it, "All agree in representing the soil of that island as the most fertile in the world."[84] One writer trumpeted that a man could attend to three acres of coffee trees easily, leaving plenty of free time for other crops. Not only was coffee touted as simple to grow, but in some areas, little cultivation was necessary since trees were "breaking down with coffee."[85] And according to some reports, coffee rotted on the trees because it was so plentiful.[86] Cocoa, another cash crop, was also straightforward to grow, "requiring very little labour [or] attendance."[87] Fruit trees were also described as effortless because these trees yielded "spontaneously."[88] Even more mundane products supposedly grew at an accelerated and explosive rate. One acre of potatoes yielded five hundred bushels of potatoes, four times as much as an acre of potatoes in the United States would produce.[89] An acre of corn could yield three different corn harvests in one year, while wheat and rice were considered "equally productive."[90] To what extent African Americans believed these descriptions of Haiti as a paradise remained to be seen. They were reported as fact and meant to attract large numbers of potential farmers and cultivators. These reports were also meant to ease apprehensions of those who were unfamiliar with cultivation and its potential challenges. The ease, fertility, and availability of Haitian land as depicted in these newspaper reports certainly would have attracted potential migrants.

These rhapsodic claims to our modern ears sound inflated and overblown, but this sort of language was common among those who sought to promote migration. In Gottfried Duden's *Report*, descriptions of the land and the settlement process fostered such ideas of Missouri that he set the stage for tens of thousands to seek out this brand-new state. In a series of thirty-six letters written as reports, Duden claimed that the "immense area, the mild climate, the splendid river connections, the ... unhindered communication, ... the perfect safety of person and property, together with very low taxes," made his corner of Missouri the place for German speakers seeking a new life. His depiction of the settlement process only further enhanced the Edenic view of the United States: any newcomer could "roam through the beautiful countryside for hundreds of miles to select land with a cover of wood and meadows in accord with one's own desires." In addition, Duden waxed lyrical about the soil and its richness; it was so rich that he claimed fertilization would only be required every one hundred years.[91]

Among the Irish and British settlers in Canada, similar descriptions of life in the New World reached audiences that remained home. One of the Irish migrants who went out with the first group of 568 attested in a newspaper report to the treatment and settlement process: the migrants received "bedding and blankets and all kinds of carpenters' tools and farming utensils." Not only did they receive these expensive and essential items, but they also testified to each family having a log house built within two days of their arrival. They expected soon to receive a cow, which had been promised to each family; a cow was an important element to these first settlers because of the milk and meat it could provide.[92] These initial reports, such as the one from the Irish settler, played an important role in popularizing the migration and settlement and showed immediate results when thousands more lined up to accept Wilmot-Horton's offer of assisted migration. For those who wrote positive letters about the migration and settlement under the Petworth Committee, their letters became central features in the marketing materials used to promote the project. While the desire for land motivated many of these Petworth migrants, there were many who chose to work for others first, such as the Leggett brothers, who found that room, board, and monthly wages were the usual arrangement. As one observer noted, "A man will get more a month here with his board, than in England without."[93] Regarding the quality of the land, settler Stephen Goatcher described it as "the very best quality," with "not one stone to be found; it's black loam." Wheat and Indian corn, he wrote, grow "very well."[94] Regardless of where you settled, "pheasants and hares, and thousands of pigeons," as well as "cherries in the woods, and currants, gooseberries and nuts," could be had for any to have.[95] As for the people he found, he described them as being "very fond of the English": "[they] are very kind to us."[96] Laborers were in high demand, and many settlers reported how they had been offered work along the way in towns and cities they passed. Richard Neal, a bricklayer, reported how he was offered more than five shillings a day in Montreal. Neal, like Goatcher, pointed out that many new roads were expected to be cleared "before long," thus allowing crops and finished goods to be transported.[97] These letters and the descriptions within them of the life and countryside to be found in Canada gave people back in England a sense of what to expect. Much of the content of the Canadian letters—the wages, the accessibility of food, and the quality of the land—would be familiar to those who sought out a new life in Haiti. In addition to these essential elements, the marketability of the crops grown featured far more in the Haitian promotional materials than in the Canadian materials.

Repeated references were made in the newspaper reports on Haiti to how much certain crops demanded on the open market. These articles eagerly calculated the sizeable returns to be made cultivating cash crops. If, for example, coffee sold for ten cents a pound, then expected profits cleared would be as much as $1,500.[98] For the average Philadelphia African American, this amount was almost ten times what they held in property.[99] Tobacco also produced profits; by one estimate, $600 worth could be harvested on three acres.[100] Even corn and potatoes yielded substantial profits: fifty cents a bushel for corn and twenty cents a bushel for potatoes.[101]

As an experienced farmer, Butler was exactly the sort of settler Boyer most wanted to target. Butler knew that even with fertile land and a reliable market, every individual crop brought its own challenges and every climate and soil their own peculiarities. Although he was probably familiar with growing corn and potatoes, his unfamiliarity with coffee surely gave him pause: could he and his family be successful in Haiti growing coffee? Some of Butler's qualms were probably alleviated when he learned that Boyer instituted an education program for neophyte cultivators of coffee, dispatching an adviser to demonstrate techniques and tricks.[102] Having an adviser who could provide hands-on experience and look out for his interests may have eliminated any of Butler's remaining reservations. How widespread these advisers were for consultation and how often they were available was not reported.

Another feature of Boyer's plan—sharecropping—was highly advertised and celebrated in American newspapers as the best method for inexperienced settlers to learn farming. At the time, commentators remarked on the number of urban dwellers who sought work in Haiti as cultivators. For those who were toiling away in America, such as Edward Anderson, a twenty-four-year-old "laborer," and Ann Holland, a twenty-two-year-old "adventurer," accounts of the riches to be made in Haiti were powerful incentive indeed.[103] Cropping was effectively on-the-job training because it gave inexperienced African Americans knowledge of cultivation techniques without the enormous risks or responsibilities involved in farm ownership. The American croppers worked for a year or two on a large plantation in exchange for one-fourth of the harvest. In addition, after one year of sharecropping, a cropper became eligible for three acres of land. Settlers without money could begin immediately as sharecroppers since food, lodging, and tools including horses, mules, plows, and hoes were provided by the landowner to the workers. Because so little initial investment was required of the laborers, Boyer requested that the settlers repay the government for their passage at the end of six months.

A Presbyterian minister in Philadelphia, Benjamin F. Hughes, like many of his fellow travelers, envisioned Haiti providing economic opportunities. The economic incentive, in this case, outweighed concerns about religious tolerance. Hearing of the vast fortunes made from trade and of the assistance Boyer was prepared to give American settlers instilled in Hughes a desire to travel to Haiti.[104] Hughes felt pinched from a shortage of funds and had resigned his appointment in the First African Church in Philadelphia to "engage in mercantile pursuits" elsewhere. He explained that "the support" he received was insufficient "to sustain him."[105] In the meantime, Hughes took an appointment offered by the New York Missionary Society in the summer of 1824 to go to Haiti.[106] Judging by his reports, he never pursued missionary activities during his stay, as Boyer had clearly prohibited Protestant evangelical activities.[107] Hughes probably thought he could do both: cater to the spiritual needs of the American settlers and pursue his own merchant activities.[108] These Presbyterian settlers, he calculated, could obtain enough wealth in Haiti to sustain a minister. If not, he could always maintain himself with commercial activities of his own.

Not all emigrants went for profit, however. Another Philadelphian, Dr. Belfast Burton, may have seen the article in the *National Gazette* that complained of the shortage of doctors in the Haitian countryside. The advertisement stated, "The number of physicians in Hayti is below what is called for by the amount of our population, those whom we have are, for most part, residents in our cities."[109] Perhaps because of the paucity of doctors, Burton moved to Samana, in the newly incorporated Spanish region. The town was also the destination of fellow Philadelphians moving to work in the shipyards. Burton's services as a doctor would be needed in a new place with a different climate.[110] Another consideration for Burton would have been language skills, since a doctor required some proficiency. Did Burton know Spanish? Perhaps he did, but there is no evidence.

The way Haiti was featured in the newspaper reports of the day, it offered African Americans a place where they could fulfill economic and social dreams of advancement. But it was also a place where equality for people with a black skin existed and, for some, a place to avenge injustices through standing in arms with a black army. As the summer of 1824 drew to a close, the African American community recognized a historic opportunity in Haiti: an opportunity to contribute to an independent black nation through their labor and skills; an opportunity to support the defense of that nation against its former colonial power; an opportunity to provide an economic alternative to slavery; and an opportunity to give themselves and their children a better life. Boyer's second great attempt at strengthening ties with the U.S. was in full swing.

6 / Haitian Realities and the Emigrants' Return

On arrival in Haiti, many emigrants such as Daniel Copelain, Aaron Blandon, and Abel Reed wrote glowing letters about Haiti to friends and family back in the United States. Copelain described how he had purchased 147 acres of land in Samana and expected within three months to gather "about two thousand weight of coffee." He declared, "I am very well satisfied with the country."[1] Samana, a small port town in the former eastern Santo Domingo, received approximately 460 American settlers by April 1825, many of whom expected to work in the newly established shipyards while others grew coffee. Blandon, a Philadelphia settler, lived near Cape Haitian, where more than eight hundred other Americans had settled. He anticipated growing coffee in the mountainous area called Plaisance and wrote how "thankful" he was "that a kind Providence" had "opened this door."[2] Reed, who landed in Port-au-Prince, was one of four thousand American settlers who made the capital home. In the Port-au-Prince region, cultivators mainly grew cotton and coffee, although some sugar planting continued. Reed wrote of meeting President Boyer and the warm reception he and his fellow Americans had received, noting how Boyer had taken each of their hands as a father would "the hands of his children" after a long absence.[3]

Boyer watched the progress of American settlement closely and had every reason to greet the settlers so warmly. The success of his grand stratagem hung in the balance—would opening up Haiti as an emigrant destination bring the U.S. to the diplomatic bargaining table? By 1824, Boyer's relationship with France had hit a diplomatic impasse when France demanded that Haiti become a tributary state in exchange for a formal peace treaty. After twenty years of self-rule, these were unacceptable—and disrespectful—terms. Boyer cut off further diplomatic talks with France. Rumors persisted that French officials contemplated using military intervention to force Haiti to some agreement or even designed to retake the colony.[4] For these reasons, Boyer watched the American settlement process to see if it would produce the expected diplomatic thaw in Washington.

* * *

When Boyer proposed the emigration project, he had hoped to disperse large numbers of emigrants evenly throughout the island.[5] Instead of one thousand emigrants landing in Port-au-Prince as expected, more than four thousand did.[6] The unanticipated influx of people created a scarcity of nearby and available government lands. Boyer had envisioned that most Americans would take up his offer to farm government lands, under which each person was entitled to three acres. He had made this the most attractive of his offers, since these farmers—unlike emigrants seeking other situations—would not have to repay the cost of their passage.[7] But emigrants who arrived in Port-au-Prince refused to take these lands, which were thirty to forty miles away from the city, too far for many Americans who had envisioned a smoother transition from urban to rural life. As the Americans poured into Port-au-Prince, government lands within proximity of the city were quickly exhausted, and rather than live in isolation, many Americans chose to become sharecroppers.

Long before the American settlers began arriving, sharecropping had become the most common labor system in postindependence Haiti. It had become the default method because Haitian landowners had little cash to pay wages but still needed a workforce. Cropping agreements gave a share of the crop (usually between one-third and one-half) to be divided between the landowner and the laborers. Planters hoped to exert control over the workers and to keep them motivated by sharing a part of the crop at the end of the season. In addition to the crop, landowners supplied lodging, tools, medical services, and sometimes food as part of the labor contract.

To the Americans in Port-au-Prince, sharecropping had other advantages besides ease of access to the city. It gave emigrants with no experience an opportunity to learn farming without the risk or responsibility that working their own land entailed. And for Americans who arrived without tools or the money to buy them, it gave these neophytes an entrée to the farmer's life. One group of settlers, for example, agreed to sharecrop for the promise of "horses, jacks, mules, carts and ploughs, and all farming utensils."[8]

For others, sharecropping may have been prompted by a more short-term problem—hunger. In addition to flour, rice, corn, bread, coffee, and salted fish, Boyer promised the emigrants beef and pork rations as part of their four-month supply of government provisions. In reality, however, many never received these provisions of meat. Regardless of wealth, meat—whether salted pork, sausage, or pickled beef—was a staple of most Americans' diets and was served at most meals in the United States. Emigrants deprived of the staple likely hungered for such victuals. James Lee, who lived in the Cape Haitian region, complained how he and his fellow Americans "neither tasted nor saw a piece of meat."[9] Another emigrant reported that emigrants had grumbled about the scarcity of meat in Haiti.[10] One group of settlers, after being promised hogs and chickens, plus a share of the sugar and coffee crop, agreed to work plantation lands located ten miles outside Port-au-Prince.[11]

Some Americans received in their agreements the entire crop the first year and then shared the crop with the owner for the subsequent years. One American group appeared to have negotiated a good deal, for they received everything grown the first year and, for the subsequent years, half the cane and coffee.[12] Another group of emigrants worked for Madame Granville, the mother of Jonathas Granville, Boyer's representative in America. This group negotiated taking the entire crop for the first two years, while the third year they would split half the coffee and cane crop with Madame Granville. This arrangement was attractive, as more than forty emigrants took up her offer.[13] These lucrative agreements show that the emigrants were not going into sharecropping work purely out of desperation.

Unfortunately for the emigrants in the Port-au-Prince region, where the vast majority of the settlers lived, the situation became dire. This area was hit by an "unprecedented" drought in the winter of 1825. The drought, reportedly the worst seen in sixty years, caused streams and rivers to run dry all over the region.[14] Because of the drought, many emigrants were unable to grow and ready their own stockpiles of food once government supplies ended. Even those settlers who had negotiated food provisions as part of their contracts were affected because many plantation owners reneged on the agreements, throwing the settlers off their lands when the government provisions ran out. These landowners calculated that the crops yields were too skimpy and food too short to warrant the expenditure on the workers.[15] This situation left many settlers without food, work, or homes by early spring.

The drought also affected those who took up government lands. Although the documents do not reveal how many or which emigrants settled these lands, we can assume that some families such as the Butlers, the Paschals, and the Connors, all designated as "farmers," chose to farm their own lands.[16] Upon arrival, these experienced farmers probably began growing food provisions such as corn, potatoes, bananas, and other fruits in preparation for the time when their provisions of food ended. With such a severe drought, they, too, must have faced food shortages.

Without food, shelter, or the means to support themselves, many emigrants drifted back to Port-au-Prince in search of employment and sustenance. Perhaps as a result of the drought, the cost of food in Haiti in 1825 was extraordinarily high. While a bushel of corn could be bought for about ten cents in the United States, corn bushels in Haiti ranged between fifty cents and one dollar.[17] Many items such as wheat and corn meal—staples of most emigrants' diet—continued to be imported, so these too were expensive—so expensive, in fact, that one emigrant suggested in a letter, "Those who are able, ought to bring with them flour, and all kinds of dry goods, for they will more than double their money here [in Haiti]."[18]

For the American settlers in Port-au-Prince, the difficulties continued mounting. A smallpox epidemic swept through the city and region in the winter of 1825, eventually spreading to Cape Haitian.[19] Haitians blamed the epidemic on the American emigrants, who, they said, had carried the disease from the U.S. A Philadelphia group that arrived in Port-au-Prince in December 1824 reportedly introduced the epidemic.[20] More than forty thousand people perished in the vicinity of Port-au-Prince, while in Cape Haitian, more than 10 percent of the city's population died.[21]

Although it is impossible to say whether the Philadelphia settlers commenced the epidemic (the ship had been quarantined), an American emigrant likely introduced the dreaded disease, since public health officials in both New York and Philadelphia had battled smallpox earlier that winter. In New York, 394 black New Yorkers became infected with smallpox, and 113 died from the disease.[22] In Philadelphia, eighty-seven African Americans contracted smallpox, and of those, sixty-six died.[23] As the incubation period for the disease lasted up to two weeks, those who were infected and contagious often did not realize they were ill until fevers, chills, and blisters emerged.[24] American settlers traveled in cramped, crowded ships for up to three weeks at a time, conditions ripe for the spread of smallpox. A sneeze, a cough, or a touch was all the microbe required for transmission. The public image of emigrants as smallpox carriers may explain why the residents of Port-au-Prince, who had been "hospitable in the extreme" and had rendered "every assistance in their power, for the comfort of the emigrants," as one report put it, were unwilling six months later to host Americans in their homes.[25]

The disease, however, should not have had such a devastating effect among the inhabitants in Haiti since smallpox vaccinations had been administered extensively there in the 1810s.[26] Vaccination—a newer and more effective approach than inoculation—was meant to eradicate the disease and should have stopped its deadly path. Unfortunately, the smallpox epidemic of 1825 revealed that the Haitian vaccination project had been made up of "spurious" viral material, which gave recipients no immunity to the disease.[27] The island inhabitants' false belief that they were vaccinated may have discouraged caution and inadvertently hastened the spread of the disease.

By late winter, large numbers of Americans began to flee Port-au-Prince and Boyer's experiment. The drought, coupled with the smallpox epidemic, dashed hopes, both for them and for Boyer. By the end of March 1825, two hundred emigrants had returned to the United States.[28] These emigrants may have wanted to leave much earlier in the year, but the dangers of a drastic change in temperature—jumping from the extreme heat of Haiti to the bitter cold wintertime of the northern United States—certainly played into considerations. Also, the ports of Baltimore and Philadelphia often froze for months during the winter, thus delaying returns. Among these early returns were the large families, including the Butlers, the Connors, and the Pachals.[29] The drought and the cost of food were undoubtedly harsh on families with so many mouths to feed.[30]

But the Port-au-Prince region was not the only challenging environment. In Samana, John Cromwell, the Baltimore ship carpenter named King, and the other Philadelphia and Baltimore shipbuilders who had expected to find a bustling shipyard instead found themselves in a veritable ghost town. Boyer had changed his mind about developing a shipyard in Samana, leaving shipwrights, ship carpenters, caulkers, and others adrift with very little means of subsistence. In one of Jonathas Granville's first acts back in Haiti after his stay in the United States, he traveled to Samana to distribute money, clothes, and supplies to the settlers there, spending almost $400.[31] While there, he gave John Cromwell and Thomas Robertson enough money to give them a "start at store keeping" and goods worth over ninety dollars.[32] Philip Bell, Francis Duperton, and Francie Mitchell, as well as several women, received money from Granville.[33] Although these emigrants received assistance, many others did not. Many chose to return to the United States rather than face any further hardships in a foreign country. Boyer was keenly aware that negative publicity would be damaging for his diplomatic efforts, and he paid for many of these first Americans' passages back to the U.S. Whether these Samana settlers were among the two hundred who returned is unknown.

Despite Boyer's initial efforts to manage the fallout of these mass returns and the negative publicity they guaranteed the project, he declared that Haiti was no longer going to financially underwrite American emigrants' passage to the island after June 1825. Boyer explained that his decision was prompted by evidence of widespread American swindling. He claimed that American ship captains, in concert with the emigrants, arrived in Haitian ports only with the intention of receiving the passenger money, and then ship, captain, and settlers would promptly return to the United States, pocketing the money. He decried the actions of the captain and passengers of the *Olive Branch* as one example of such duplicitous behavior. That ship allegedly had spent only three days in port, without the passengers ever even disembarking. Then the ship and passengers sailed away.[34] Certainly, such activities angered Boyer, but there were other considerations that likely prompted the president's decision.

More tellingly, American recognition seemed no closer to becoming a reality than it had before the emigration project began. The American Colonization Society continued to resist Haitian emigration, and publications continued to attack the project and Boyer, calling him a despot.[35] After six months of spending a great deal of Haitian money—more than $300,000—Boyer's gamble of obtaining recognition through emigration looked like a bust.[36] He likely chose to end the project early and save what he could of his country's treasure.[37]

Another factor in this decision to end the financing of American settlement was the thaw in French diplomatic relations. Boyer's negotiations with France over recognition were making headway in early 1825, and these talks obviated some of the diplomatic motives for African American emigration. These talks and the costs of the settlement project prompted Boyer to conclude that financing American emigration was no longer in his nation's economic interest. And Boyer needed to save what he could of his country's treasure because in signing the peace treaty with France, he agreed to pay an indemnity that hobbled Haiti's economic and national development for decades.

At first, news of the French and Haitian agreement was welcomed, as Haiti's independence had finally been acknowledged.[38] Celebrations filled the streets, with cheering crowds calling out, "Vive la France, vive Haiti, vive Charles X, vive Boyer!" Boyer spoke before the Port-au-Prince crowds, declaring, "[The French have] consecrate[d] the legitimacy of your emancipation," and he predicted that the nation's "commerce and agriculture will now be greatly extended. The arts and sciences, which rejoice in peace, will be highly improved [and will] . . . embellish your new situation with all the benefits of civilization."[39] Commentators seconded Boyer's predictions, stating that the treaty would bring "new vigor to the agriculturalists, and inspire with new enterprise the merchants [in Haiti]."[40] Everything seemed within Haiti's reach now that the French threat had been neutralized.

The news of the peace treaty was greeted in the United States with celebrations, as the African American community commemorated the event with dinners, speeches, toasts, and songs. One group of Boston celebrants believed that now the two nations would soon "be united by [a] treaty of Amity and Friendship."[41] But as news got out about the agreed-on indemnity and its exorbitant costs, expectations about Haiti's ability to pay it were mixed. One American noted that the indemnity "change[d] the whole aspect of things" and was "so degrading and so dangerous" to Haitian interests that it would create far greater "injury than advantage."[42] Niles, always the optimist, believed that "the purchase money to France will be easily paid. . . . It was already in hand, waiting for the purpose."[43]

Under the terms of the treaty, the young nation was on the hook for 150 million francs to be paid in five installments of 30 million.[44] The first installment was due January 1826, six months from the signing of the treaty. Whether Boyer remained optimistic about paying off the first installment of the indemnity is unclear.[45] He negotiated a loan of 24 million francs from a French bank, leaving the remaining 6 million to be obtained. He collected the remainder of the money by levying additional taxes on patents, higher duties on coffee exports, and a new tax called "the contribution tax," a five-dollar head tax on every inhabitant in the nation.[46] These taxes were the only feasible way to meet the repayments.

In Boyer's rush to pin down sources of money, he instantly raised the patent tax—a form of business license—on all Haitians and their business partners.[47] The effect of these higher taxes on the American emigrants can be seen immediately. For example, Belfast Burton, who worked as a doctor and sold medicine on the side, faced a tax increase of fifty gourdes—as much as thirty-five U.S. dollars—for just the right to sell medicine in 1825. This tax was in addition to the one levied on his professional license. To practice his profession, he paid an additional twenty-four gourdes, or as much as seventeen dollars, a year.[48] Burton may have calculated that it cost too much to be a practicing doctor in Haiti and chose to return to the United States in December 1825, days before the new fees were to be assessed.[49] Accompanying Burton were a shoemaker, a hatter, joiners, farmers, milliners, mechanics, laborers, and traders. They all set sail in ships bound for the United States in late 1825 and early 1826. The timing of these artisans' return suggests that the new taxes on business were a factor. Perhaps Boyer would have shown more effort in appeasing American settlers if diplomatic matters with France had not taken precedent, because regardless of what happened internationally, Haiti still needed the Americans' labor.

Another cost-saving solution—decommissioning soldiers—became jeopardized when Spain began to make its own threat toward Haiti. Just as Boyer began to reduce the size of the army, Spain demanded monetary compensation for the loss of Santo Domingo.[50] The Spanish negotiations became so heated that the Spanish Crown threatened to attack the island. This situation put an end to Haiti's demilitarization. It also reopened the drain on the treasury and undercut Boyer's plans to pay the indemnity to France.

To make matters worse, the Haitian treasury saw additional losses to its operating funds in 1825 and 1826 because of a lower-than-expected coffee crop. In 1824, Haitians sold forty-four million pounds of coffee, but that dropped 20 percent in 1825 to thirty-six million pounds of coffee and remained near this level in 1826.[51] Although the drought certainly must have played into the lower production levels in 1825, by 1826, the drought had lifted. Why had production levels not increased with the new American labor force? American laborers failed to boost production because of the vagaries of coffee cultivation. For emigrants who worked as farmers and sharecroppers, cultivating coffee turned out to be more demanding than had been reported in America, requiring larger reserves of capital, greater physical demands, and a longer commitment of time. It was also far less lucrative than they had been led to believe by boosters in both the United States and Haiti.

After the Haitian Revolution, many coffee plantation lands lay neglected and became overgrown with weeds and shrubs. These coffee trees also required pruning and separating—backbreaking work—as many closely planted trees had grown into tangled groves during the previous decades. Even if a farmer had been fortunate and the trees on his land did not require extensive clearing, weeding was a constant chore in the tropics, where there was no killing frost. In addition to these tasks, farmers had to harvest the beans, dry them, and then bag the crop for the market. In the Caribbean, the gathering of coffee for the harvest coincided with the rainy season, adding torrential rains to what was an arduous job at the best of times. Farmers who failed to take the proper precautions in drying their coffee in Haiti's wet conditions risked losing the entire crop to mold. The Americans, new to the processing of coffee and inexperienced with its handling, very likely jeopardized their crop in many instances.[52]

Furthermore, cultivating coffee was not as profitable as many emigrants had been told. If the coffee trees were in their prime, they produced as much as four pounds a tree, or 19,500 pounds of coffee per three acres. This yield represents the highest level for productive trees on Haiti, but coffee trees did not produce at these levels indefinitely—they usually passed their peak after sixty years. Because many Haitian coffee trees had been planted in the 1760s, by the 1820s, they were past their prime. These older trees yielded less per acre. And if the Americans received land with immature coffee trees, these trees could not produce annually the four pounds per tree of a prime tree. Immature coffee trees normally required up to five years to reach their prime and bear a full coffee crop. Most Americans likely saw considerably less yield than the prime output from their three acres—and far less in profits.

In addition to these problems with production, the coffee market was down, compounding Boyer's revenue gathering. So dramatic was the price decline that coffee sold at half its 1822 value in 1826.[53] Coffee had sold for as much as thirteen cents a pound in the early 1820s, but by 1825, the bottom had fallen out of the market, with the crop selling between three and six cents a pound. For example, the estimated 19,500 pounds of coffee obtained from three acres was only worth $585 when calculated at three cents a pounds, far less than the $1,500 touted in American newspapers.

Coffee was the blood supply for the entire Haitian economy. As an American who settled in Jeremie noted, all business stood still until the coffee crop sold.[54] With lower prices on the world market, this meant that Haitian coffee bought far fewer imported goods. The effect of the drop in coffee production and prices could already be seen in the stores and shops of the island in the spring of 1825. One American was struck by the lack of goods available and commented, "You can hardly look into a shop or purchase an article of any description."[55] Without coffee, the economy was anemic. Overall, commercial trade fell between 30 and 50 percent between 1824 and 1826.[56]

In a drastic attempt to jump-start productivity, Boyer enacted the Code Rural. Put into effect on May 1, 1826, the series of laws created a class of forced laborers on plantations.[57] With the exception of landowners, government and military officers, and artisans and shopkeepers, no laborer was allowed to leave his or her assigned plantation without a pass, or he or she was subject to either a fine or imprisonment.[58] The Code Rural not only limited the movement of the workers; it also limited the prospects of the plantation cultivators' children. These children could not attend school or become apprentices without the permission of the local justice of the peace—taking away parental control and one of the hallmarks of freedom. The plantations were also assigned military officers who controlled the movements and enforced the day-to-day schedule of the workers. For those who had survived Christophe's former kingdom, these rules and regulations would have been familiar, as he had imposed similar laws on his subjects with the Code Henry. Louverture and Dessalines had also implemented such laws during their rule.

While the regulations forbade the use of physical force by these officers, instances of physical punishment and violence were common.[59] One such incident involved an administrator of Boyer's own staff who swung a cocomacac—a heavy jointed cane—with enough force to knock out the eye of a seeming "loiterer," an agricultural laborer found not working.[60] Reminiscent of the slave era, these new labor laws and the enforcement techniques that accompanied them caused massive discontent among the populace.

Unsurprisingly, these new farming measures, coupled with the dissatisfaction over the French indemnity, fueled great instability on the island. Popular unrest was reported in Cape Haitian almost immediately after the terms of the indemnity were made public. Other civil disturbances broke out intermittently throughout the island, even in the republican strongholds of Port-au-Prince and Aux Cayes.[61] Despite Boyer's attempts to quell them, the rioting continued. So did calls for Boyer's resignation and the repudiation of the French treaty. One American predicted that Haitian citizens would break out in "revolution" if the treaty was not renegotiated.[62] In a later report, another observer expected that Boyer would resign his "post by request," because the discontent had become so widespread.[63]

These violent outbreaks of civil discord may even have involved some American settlers. John Allen, the son of AME bishop Richard Allen, was rumored to have been shot in Haiti. Little is known about how the rumor began, but it created such a stir within the Philadelphia community that the Colored Haytien Emigration Society of Philadelphia printed a statement in its 1825 publication of *Information for the Free People of Colour* refuting the shooting.[64] That such a rumor started at all demonstrates the American perception of a violent breakdown in the country's law and order.

The popular dissatisfaction with the French indemnity also raises questions about the settlers' perception of Boyer and Haiti's commitment to black independence. Was Haiti truly independent in the face of such a payment? Had Boyer sacrificed too much in accepting such an agreement? The Americans who remained in Haiti may have found the debates over Haiti's independence, coupled with the Code Rural's ruthless enforcement, difficult to reconcile with their expectations of Haiti as a black land of the free. Worse, Boyer agreed to a British provision that a runaway slave "from the British colonies" who made his or her way to Haiti would be restored to the British colonial authorities.[65] What happened to the Haiti where all worked together for the unity and prosperity of the black race?

Among U.S. abolitionists, the Code Rural also made Haiti's involvement in the free produce movement problematic, since by most standards, the workers of Haiti were now forced labor. When Boyer planned the distribution of the emigrants, he anticipated more than a thousand American settlers cultivating cotton around Port-au-Prince and Gonaives, the two centers of cotton cultivation.[66] These cotton cultivators were now likely subject to the Code Rural, which imposed laws on all plantation laborers.[67] Haiti had gone from a dream to a nightmare for these Americans who had anticipated working for the destruction of slavery but instead found themselves facing slave-like conditions.

As for the manufacturing aspects of the free produce movement, Haiti's economy was clearly unprepared for such enterprises. As one American reported, there was minimal manufacturing of cloth: "There are no cloths made in the island, either of cotton, silk, or wool, not even of the home-made family manufacture. The spindle and loom are hardly known in the island."[68] Most Haitian cloth came from British manufacturers and merchants, so even if some enterprising American individuals had sought to develop textile manufacturing, it remained a difficult task, since banking was unknown in Haiti until the end of the 1820s.[69] And the economic havoc that the French treaty wrought on the island's already vulnerable financial state took most available cash out of the system.

John Allen and other entrepreneurs realized that their plans were unworkable in the new Haitian economic and social environment. Because of the radical alterations in Haiti's social and economic outlook, settlers such as Allen, expecting to capitalize on their skills and connections, thought it best to return to the United States. Allen left Port-au-Prince on September 8, 1826, on a ship bound for Philadelphia that also carried two returning American seamstresses, Harriet and

Rachel Webster.[70] The return of artisans and skilled laborers reflects Haiti's lack of support for new businesses. It also reflects the tough competition from already-established Haitian enterprises. According to Charles Mackenzie, Port-au-Prince was well stocked with "all the ordinary tradesmen, such as tailors, [and] shoe-makers."[71]

And yet through all of these disappointments and thwarted expectations, there were some skilled emigrants who expressed contentment with Haiti. R.M.S. from Philadelphia, who settled in Port-au-Plat on the northern coast of the former colony of Santo Domingo, reported how he found work as a journeyman for an Englishman almost as soon as he arrived in the port. His one complaint was that he wished he had his own set of tools because if he did, he could have made a considerable fortune. Even so, working as a journeyman, he was expecting to make between fifteen and twenty dollars a week. He also admitted that knowing a smattering of French had been of "great service."[72] His story suggests that skilled workers could build satisfactory lives in this small port town and others like it, such as Samana.

The emigrants who settled in Samana, the region on the northern coast of the present-day Dominican Republic, left the most discernible trail in the historical record. An African American community endured on the isolated peninsula throughout the nineteenth century. Because the United States was interested in acquiring the region as a coaling station in the 1870s, a commission to investigate and report on the region for the U.S. Congress was sent to gauge its suitability.[73] Frederick Douglass was among the members of the commission, suggesting that the delegation was not purely commercial in its mission. The report, titled *Report of the Commission of Inquiry to Santo Domingo* (1871), details the customs of the inhabitants and the geography of the peninsula. The commission interviewed members of the community and made estimates on the number of African Americans who lived there. By these estimates, about 150 of the 200 who had traveled on the *Four Sons* from the United States remained and made Samana their home. The families who stayed retained many of their original names, as can be seen in the storefronts and small businesses of the area: King, Kelly, Willmore, Coplin, Green, Johnson, Shephard, and Jones.[74] As Samana was accessible only by boat from the rest of the island, the Americans were not assimilated, and retaining the English language, African American cuisine ("johnnycakes" shortbread may have come to the Caribbean from the southern U.S. by way of Samana), religious affiliation to Protestantism (the Wesleyans provided a minister when the AME church could not), and their identity as Americans.[75] As recently as the 2000s, linguists have detected speech patterns among the remaining Anglophones in Samana that are closely related to those of antebellum African Americans. The colony, for that is what the Samana community became, deliberately maintained this isolation and worked to "preserve [their] feelings as Americans."[76] In addition to this abiding affiliation to the United States and the English language, the commissioners' report reveals that many of the original African American families continued to farm the original allotments distributed by Boyer in the 1820s. They also had received title to them, just as Boyer had promised. One family had even expanded on its original fifteen acres over the half century and had acquired more than three hundred acres of farm land. As one Samana resident observed, those of American descent are "the foremost men in the settlement." Another commentator noted that the American colonists "are the most intelligent and well-to-do" and that "nearly every one of these colonists has done well."[77]

Unfortunately, most American settlers did not fare as well as those in Samana. Confronted by a changing economic and social system, Americans also experienced firsthand the gap between de jure and de facto political rights in Haiti. The Haitian constitution guaranteed to all black-skinned males over the age of twenty-one after one year of residency the right to vote in Haitian elections. African American men eagerly anticipated exercising their right to vote and could do so in the December 1826 election of the Haitian Congress. A group of Americans living in Port-au-Prince not only prepared to vote, but they also put up a fellow settler, a Methodist minister, as a candidate. According to one report, when they approached the polling booth, both the minister and the rest of the Americans were "entered in at one door and civilly handed out of the opposite one, without having been allowed a solitary vote."[78] Not only were the Americans denied the right of suffrage, but it became clear that the election as a whole was a sham. According to another report, no one knew who was running until "after the election was over," when the "elected" deputies took office.[79] There were other instances in which the settlers could not exercise their full citizenship rights. Jury duty, which had been denied to black New Yorkers regardless of their freehold status, was also withheld in Haiti. Although legislation mandating trial by jury passed in 1826, the system was never utilized by the Haitian courts.[80] The reality of political life in Haiti undermined many settlers' view of the island as their "black republic." Here, they were denied the privilege of voting so brazenly as to be reminiscent of life in the United States. In circumventing the Americans' vote, the Haitians revealed their reluctance to uphold the promise of Haiti as a black nation for all descendants of Africa. This black nation that had agreed to give them equality, to guarantee them citizenship, and to welcome them as brothers and sisters failed to deliver on any of these promises.

After strenuous efforts were made to pay the first installment of the indemnity, the Haitian economy was in ruins by the spring of 1826. The government issued a decree on April 1 that explained that "current circumstances" demanded that those who owed money to the government "pay back their debts." If the debtors should fail to repay within one month's time, their land would be seized and sold.[81] Whether this applied to American settlers is unclear.[82] No mention is made in any emigrant letter or newspaper report about this Haitian decree applying to the American settlers.

By December 1826, American newspapers reported on the ominous change in the Haitian situation since the signing of the peace treaty. The *Eastern Argus* described how "a few years since, [Haiti] was in a flourishing condition, both as respect its commerce and fiscal concerns. . . . This change is attributed to the artful terms of the recognition of Hayti, by the French government."[83] In the same edition, another correspondent from Cape Haitian conceded that "all confidence is at an end" and that "the commerce of the country is all but annihilated."[84] Boyer had even been forced to issue additional paper money to help offset the loss of currency.[85] According to the *National Gazette*, Haiti had never been "in such distress as at this moment."[86] Later that month, another report in the *National Gazette* stated that the inhabitants of Haiti were experiencing "an unprecedented state of poverty and misery."[87]

Because many American settlers earned so little money during their stay and had spent whatever savings they arrived with, they were forced to remain in Haiti until many had gathered enough money to finance their return passage.[88] This situation took some emigrants years to negotiate, while others never did. The Passenger List for Philadelphia shows that at least one emigrant, William

Rop, financed his return by working as a sailor aboard the schooner *Amelia*.[89] How others financed their return passage is unknown. Some emigrants such as James Lee, the Cape Haitian emigrant who complained of the lack of meat, reported that "he made his escape on the 28th of November [1825], but was compelled to leave his family behind."[90] Another settler, William Tapsico, who sailed from Jeremie in 1827, may have left his pregnant wife, Mary, until the birth of their baby, because both mother and child departed from Jeremie for Philadelphia in 1828.[91] Perhaps both men believed their earning potential was greater in the United States and thus could send for family much faster than if they had remained and then left together.[92]

It is difficult to know how many women and children who traveled back to the United States alone left behind husbands or fathers or followed them home separately.[93] William Rop's ability to finance his return trip provides clues to what happened in some circumstances. Seeking passage on a merchant ship was one method families could use to finance their return to the United States. Since many African American men possessed some experience as sailors, they likely negotiated terms with captains to receive a portion of their wages early. This money, in turn, could finance the return passage of a man's family back to the United States. According to the Passenger Lists, thirty-seven women with children sailed back to the United States without a male companion. Many of these women may have been widowed during their stay in Haiti.[94] Widowhood was widespread among women in the African American community living in America. Nearly one in six women over the age of twenty-four lived as widows in Philadelphia at this time.[95] Although the mortality rates cited in Samana disproportionately affected women and infants, as the emigrants settled in and began the hard physical labor required for farming, men likely succumbed to diseases, too.

The Passenger Lists also indicate that many children were orphaned during their sojourn in Haiti. Sailing on the schooner *Mary Ann*, George, age two, "a free black child," had no last name listed. He may have been the child of one of the several women on board, but the fact that he has no last name listed and is not described with the more common "child of" indicates his probable orphaned state.[96] There were also the Gray children, Patience and Francis, both fourteen, who traveled alone to Philadelphia without another family member, as did

Joseph Peco and Matilda Johnson, ages eight and eleven, respectively, who both departed from Cape Haitian for Philadelphia.[97] Were these children orphaned by the smallpox epidemic that hit Cape Haitian, or had their parents sent them back to the United States while they remained behind? The three sisters Clarissa, Eliza, and Lydia Edmunds perhaps were the daughters of William Edmonds, the tobacconist from New York who had sailed to Haiti on the *De Witt Clinton*.[98] That the daughters embarked without their father raises questions about his fate in Haiti. The death rate in Haiti certainly remained high, like all the Caribbean islands at this time. Charles Mackenzie, the British consul stationed in Haiti, cited the example of the French consul's family to demonstrate the high death rates. In less than two years, five of the consul's six family members were dead.[99]

In addition to the smallpox epidemic that hit the island in 1824 and 1825, settlers would have been exposed to malaria. Malaria infection, as one observer noted, was a "constant" presence in Port-au-Prince, because the shallow water near the quays allowed "all sorts of uncleanliness."[100] Even for those Americans who had survived the rigors of settlement, the return passage exposed many to the deadly disease. The specter of death did not leave the emigrants on the wharf in Haiti; it followed some on board: the two-year-old daughter of Francis and Louisa Webb, Mary Ann, died en route to Philadelphia.[101] She may have caught malaria while she and her family waited on the docks in Port-au-Prince to board the ship to return to America.

Serena Baldwin, the young New Yorker, was apparently more fortunate, because no one in her family died in Haiti or on the return passage. The Baldwin family remained in the City of Santo Domingo until 1828, when they, too, followed many of their compatriots and made their departure for New York City.[102] Although not much is known of what William Baldwin did during his stay in Haiti, his occupation was listed as a "merchant" on the Passenger List. This was a step up from his "oysterman" occupation in New York, suggesting that he tried his hand at trading, since Santo Domingo had a bustling trade in luxury wood and cattle.[103] He may have adjusted to paying seventy-five gourdes a year to be in business, but as the Haitian economy faltered and the commercial presence of American shippers declined, Baldwin would have found turning a profit ever more difficult. The British consul described how American trade declined remarkably after 1825 when France demanded as part of its treaty agreement to pay only 6 percent in trade duties, compared to the 12 percent duty the British and American traders paid. Mackenzie went on to note that in 1826, there were forty-one fewer American vessels trading than previously, while there were twenty-three additional French vessels.[104] Even if Baldwin wished to develop trade with the Caribbean neighbors, this became impossible in 1827, when Boyer again imposed an embargo on all Haitian vessels traveling to foreign ports, effectively ending trade with other Caribbean islands.[105] As for Baldwin participating and developing a trade network between Haitian ports, the high cost of coastal shipping would have made this unfeasible. In one estimate, a barreled item shipped between Cape Haitian and Port-au-Prince cost double what it would have cost to ship the same item between Port-au-Prince and New York.[106]

In all, emigrants returned home for similar reasons: unforeseen hardship, disease, and a clash between reality and what they had been led to believe. Disillusionment came in the form of a regime that failed to live up to its promise to uphold republican rights of equal citizenship and an economic landscape that discouraged rather than encouraged commercial enterprise. It was as if all the Americans' expectations were punctured one by one in Haiti's declining economy and failed diplomatic policy.

For Boyer, the emigration was an enormous disappointment. It failed to bring about the desired result—American recognition. He expended vast reserves bringing the African Americans to Haiti, only to see their impressions of his nation used against it. Very quickly, he realized that his efforts to promote Haiti's diplomatic status in Washington had been foiled again. This time, he had no one to blame but himself and, perhaps, the French negotiating team.

Although it remains impossible to know how much effort was expended in the settlement process by the Haitian government, we know that little attention was given to the settlement in the extant official state newspaper, *Le Telegraphe*. In comparison to the Petworth and Wilmot-Horton assistance programs from Great Britain, for which the organizing and settling of the migrants has been judged exceptional, Boyer's migration project was something of a failure.[107] That also seems to have been the conclusion in the American press, since little attention was given to the migration or migrants after 1826.

The story of a group of emigrants (eight families) who were still living outside Port-au-Prince in 1831 sheds light on what motivated some to endure the trials, culture shock, and hard work needed to make it in Haiti. Telling their story to a writer in the *Friend*, a Quaker publication, the group of Americans related what had befallen them in the seven years since they had settled on the island. After attempting to cultivate and make a living from farming the government lands, "expend[ing] what little capital" they possessed on "fruitless endeavors," they grew frustrated, left these lands, and moved to Port-au-Prince. There, all they found was "absolute destitution." It was in Port-au-Prince that the eight families met and chose to work with "united industry" on lands close to the city and within reach of the market. Pooling their resources, which added up to less than "10 dollars Haitian," they purchased tools; began working land abutting Boyer's personal plantation, Poids le General; and planted it with sugar cane.[108]

Sugar was far more profitable than coffee and was in demand worldwide. Sugar was also subject to less taxation than coffee. Still, it was hardly easy money—cane was also the most physically demanding of crops grown in Haiti. Unlike coffee trees, cane needed to be replanted every two years, a grueling task. Some farmers cultivated ratoons—stumps of cane that remained in the fields from the previous year's harvest. This cultivation choice was relatively rare because ratoons yielded less sugar than seed-grown sugar. If the Americans chose to plant seed-grown sugar cane, they would have dug thousands of individual holes and then inserted the seeds into the holes by hand. If they had access to a plow, it would have reduced the onerous work of holing, but plows were never widely adopted in sugar cultivation in the Caribbean.[109] Once this arduous task of seeding was complete, they then would have manured the entire field. Once the cane sprouted, the daily activity of hoeing and weeding began. When the cane reached maturity, the most taxing aspect of sugar cultivation awaited—the harvest. Cane had to be cut swiftly and then processed immediately, which meant the continual transport of the cane from the fields to the mill house. As for processing the sugar cane, the group agreed to Boyer's offer of using his sugar mills in exchange for one-quarter of the crop as payment.

The group described themselves as living in "comparative comfort and comparative wealth," which allowed them to obtain cows, pigs, poultry, and other "household wants." Although the Americans considered themselves "fortunate," they regretted the lack of schools and religious instruction available to their children. But when asked if they would return to America, the group expressed no desire to live in a country that stirred only feelings of "bitterness." To them, America held no "redeeming or consolatory hope."[110] For a few, the trials and hardships had proved worthwhile—Haiti was their home.

Conclusion

Caribbean Crossing argues that the 1820s was a critical time in the relationship between the United States and Haiti, a time when each exerted influence on the other that had the potential to change their respective histories even more radically. During this decade, Haitian President Jean-Pierre Boyer concentrated on U.S. relations in his work to improve the standing of his nation and opened up the island to African American emigrants as a gambit to strengthen his case for diplomatic recognition from the United States. Boyer's emigration plan found support among a diverse group of Americans, from abolitionists to black-community leaders to hard-nosed businessmen who all saw profit in the enterprise for different reasons. The project had a lasting effect on thousands of emigrants; on the black communities of Boston, Philadelphia, and New York (communities from which the vast majority of the emigrants originated); on Haitian-American relations; and on African American political discourse.

Haitian leaders sought a place at the international table; American free blacks sought to push back against discrimination and show the black race as an equal; antislavery whites sought to fortify a nation founded by liberated slaves; black and white businessmen wanted to open up trade; racist whites wanted to "export the race problem." The strength of this curious coalition shows that Haiti was more of a wild card in America's nineteenth-century race relations than historians have acknowledged to date. The savvy design of this coalition suggests that Boyer's aim of winning U.S. support for a black state was a viable strategic goal and not a pipe dream. Such support, of course, represented a potentially transformative gesture for contemporary slavery and race debates. The high stakes of this symbolic battle were more widely appreciated by contemporaries than scholars have detected.

The stakes of the emigration project itself were similarly high: Boyer wanted to more closely ally U.S. and Haitian interests, just as he had sought to ally the two liberated colonies' histories in the recognition debate. Free and enslaved Americans wanted to participate in the entrance of a black nation on the world stage as an equal to the white players. The emigration project perpetuated an even more unlikely coalition in the U.S. It aligned African Americans' desire to escape discrimination and economic oppression with white Americans' racially motivated efforts to remove blacks from the U.S. Boyer drew on the racial tensions in America to attract migrants and to further his (and their) goal of establishing an internationally recognized black nation for all peoples of African descent.

Caribbean Crossing tells how Haiti's early leaders sought the participation of African Americans in their nation building and saw them as an important constituency for advancing Haiti's place on the world stage. Many historians have faulted these leaders for originating the economic and political morass into which their country later slid. This is short shrift for men leading the first nation in the world to throw off slave shackles and only the second to achieve independence from colonialism. These leaders were conscious of Haiti's independence and nationhood as symbols of racial uplift but also pragmatically realized that diplomatic recognition and access to markets would determine their nation's future. All of these factors motivated Haitian leaders to seek out African American settlers.

Boyer synthesized the immigration policies of his two predecessors. The 1820s was a tough time economically and socially for African Americans living in the United States. It was also the decade when activists worked toward antislavery goals of freeing enslaved Americans rather than simply giving lip service to the idea. Boyer capitalized on these struggles by offering free passage, free land, and favorable inducements. His commitment stemmed from the belief that if enough African Americans settled on the island—first free blacks and then eventually freed southern slaves—he could expect, even demand, U.S. recognition of Haiti. For Boyer, having such an ally against France would be a deterrent to any future French invasions. His efforts succeeded in the North but foundered in the South, where Boyer's goal of attracting freed southern slaves became derailed. Despite this derailment, Boyer's savvy marketing campaign yielded a far-larger wave of migration, bringing thousands more black Americans to Haiti in the 1820s than any of his predecessors had.

To avoid hagiography, we must conclude that Boyer miscalculated the outcome of this mass migration. Neither full diplomatic recognition nor the closer economic ties materialized. As a result, Haiti became poorer; and as Haiti became poorer, black Americans stopped supporting migration. And as Haiti became poorer, white Americans saw fewer and fewer advantages to strengthening ties with the black republic. The migration project backfired spectacularly and may well have ruined Haiti's developing reputation in the U.S. The settlers themselves also damaged Boyer's goal of linking emigration and recognition. Upon arrival in Haiti, the settlers were quickly disillusioned, and many felt misled by the picture they had been presented, as seen in some of the published letters. Still, Boyer's project played a significant role in U.S. history that he could not have intended. It opened a debate about the recognition of the rights of black people to self-determination that helped to demarcate the divides in America over slavery and race.

This book is a Haitian story, cataloging Boyer's struggle to find a footing for a black nation in an era of hardening racism, slave expansion, and diplomatic isolation. But it is also an American story, about the migrants' complex reasons for leaving the U.S. and for going to Haiti. Further, the views of Haiti from U.S. contemporaries reveal much about the writers' society and the hardening sectional and racial tensions. From the emigrant letters and other sources, a glimpse of an early version of what came to be known as "activism" in the black American community is revealed. Many of the diverse men, women, and children who started new lives in Haiti were motivated as much by community and political ideals as they were by personal circumstances. They had heard sermons in support of Haitian nation building or had read pamphlets in support of self-determination. In a contemporary setting, the migration might well have been described as the culmination of a political "movement."

More than two-thirds of the settlers returned to the United States, according to some estimates. Diplomatic relations between Haiti and the U.S. hit a low point in the late 1820s, as revealed in the wrangling over the Congress of Panama, a meeting in 1826 of all the independent nations in the New World. Boyer was expected to attend and receive recognition of his nation from the newly formed Spanish American nations. American diplomats, however, refused to attend if a Haitian delegation was present, supposedly fearing that antislavery talks and Haitian recognition would dominate. U.S. policy was clearly swayed in this case by southern demands. Simón Bolívar, who had organized the conference, acceded to America's requests, leaving Haiti as the only New World nation uninvited and unacknowledged at the Panama talks. Haiti had given Bolívar arms and aid as a revolutionary in fighting Spain in the Spanish American wars of independence. That he was willing to turn his back on Haiti demonstrated the near-insurmountable odds that Boyer faced in the battle for recognition.

While Boyer failed to gain recognition through the emigration project, he moved his nation closer than any other Haitian leader had to achieving international status without any strings attached. Unfortunately, his acknowledgment from France did come with strings attached—an enormous indemnity that bankrupted the country for almost a century. One white resident of Haiti, upon learning of France's acknowledgment of the nation, found it troubling that recognition came from France rather than from the United States, writing, "when I call to mind the innumerable evils France has inflicted upon the Haytiens, it seems but a poor reparation that she should be the first to recognize their political independence." For him, if the United States had been the first country to recognize Haiti, it would have lived up to its "high toned liberality," to its "principles," and to its "national character." Because of America's own history of independence, this acknowledgment was a "measure ... which the Haytiens and the whole world had a right to expect."[1] Unfortunately, this acknowledgment from the United States failed to take place until the 1860s, when America fought its own war over slavery. White supremacists, early black nationalists, and abolitionists all had an interest in the Haitian project's success. Its failure meant that American racial issues could no longer be exported. These groups hashed out their differences for the next four decades and beyond.

In the early 1820s, American advocates for this black nation made their voices heard. For an instant, many U.S. contingents—whatever their diverse interests—seemed ready to embrace Haiti. Although the precedent of Haitian recognition might not have quelled the slavery and race debates that raged in the United States throughout the nineteenth century, it would have given black activists a basis to press for greater political and social equality. Historians have long understood that race is an ideology constructed out of the social and cultural context of a certain time.[2] Indeed, the date that diplomatic acceptance of Haiti was finally forthcoming from the United States was close to the date when President Lincoln declared the emancipation of Confederate southern slaves—1863.

As Haiti was no longer seen as a viable emigration option for most African Americans after the 1830s, it played a diminished role in African American political and economic visions. There continued to be some support in the United States for African American emigration to Haiti, as seen with Benjamin Lundy, who continued to use his newspaper, *Genius of Universal Emancipation*, to advertise Haiti's attributes into the 1830s. Despite his efforts, few took up the call. Yet Haiti's history of throwing off the double yoke of colonialism and slavery remained a powerful symbol of what the descendants of Africa could accomplish. Haiti, abandoned by its American supporters, continued its struggle to gain political and diplomatic acceptance against a hostile world and fought this battle virtually alone throughout the nineteenth century and into the twentieth. This did not have to be.

Notes

Notes to the Introduction

1. Much of the scholarly research on the intersection of Haiti and American blacks at this time looks from the Caribbean to the United States, at the émigrés who were fleeing the Haitian Revolution and its aftermath rather than vice versa. The most recent work is Ashli White, *Encountering Revolution: Haiti and the Making of the Early Republic* (Baltimore: Johns Hopkins University Press, 2010). Historians have demonstrated how news carried by refugees fleeing the revolution and sailors engaged in the carrying trade between the island and the United States found its way to slave populations along the eastern seaboard. Julius Sherrer Scott, "The Common Wind: Currents of Afro-American Communication in the Era of the Haitian Revolution" (Ph.D. diss., Duke University, 1986); and Scott, "Afro-American Sailors and the International Communication Network: The Case of Newport Bowers," in *African Americans and the Haitian Revolution: Selected Essays and Historical Documents*, ed. Maurice Jackson and Jacqueline Bacon, 25–38 (New York: Routledge, 2010); W. Jeffrey Bolster, *Black Jacks: African American Seamen in the Age of Sail* (Cambridge: Harvard University Press, 1997).

2. This New York group alone equaled the number who sailed to the American Colonization Society's African colony for the entire decade of the 1820s, showing the northern black community's enthusiasm for the project. Benjamin Hunt estimated that as many as thirteen thousand emigrated. Benjamin Hunt, *Remarks on Hayti as a Place of Settlement for Afric-Americans; and on the Mulatto as a Race for the Tropics* (Philadelphia: T. B. Pugh, 1860), 11.

3. Haytian Emigration Society of Coloured People, *Address of the Board of Managers of the Haytian Emigration Society of Coloured People, to the Emigrants Intending to Sail to the Island of Hayti, in the Brig De Witt Clinton* (New York: Mahlon Day, 1824), 4 ("pioneers"), 3 (all other quotes).

4. Ibid., 7 ("highly favoured"), 3 (all other quotes).

5. Ibid., 7.

6. Prince Hall, "A Charge" (1797), in *Pamphlets of Protest: An Anthology of Early African-American Protest Literature*, ed. Richard Newman, Patrick Rael, and Philip Lapsansky (New York: Routledge, 2001), 47.

7. Ibid.

8. Description and quotes: *Pennsylvania Correspondent* (Doylestown, Pa.), July 18, 1804; Gary Nash, *Forging Freedom: The Formation of Philadelphia's Black Community, 1720–1840* (Cambridge: Harvard University Press, 1988), 176; Shane White, "'It Was a Proud Day': African Americans, Festivals, and Parades in the North, 1741–1834," *Journal of American History* 81 (1994): 34; *Albany Centinel*, July 20, 1804. Little is known of the African American crowd's social makeup. Two men were arrested but shortly released. Their names were Benjamin Lewis and Simon Fox (Nash, *Forging Freedom*, 322n12). The next year, 1805, African Americans who assembled for the Fourth of July parade were driven from the event (Nash, *Forging Freedom*, 177).

9. Laurent Dubois, *A Colony of Citizens: Revolution and Slave Emancipation in the French Caribbean, 1787–1804* (Chapel Hill: University of North Carolina Press, 2004); Jeremy Popkin, *You Are All Free: The Haitian Revolution and the Abolition of Slavery* (New York: Cambridge University Press, 2010); John D. Garrigus, *Before Haiti: Race and Citizenship in French Saint-Domingue*, The Americas in the Early Modern Atlantic World (New York: Palgrave Macmillan, 2006).

10. Most of the following information derives from Laurent Dubois, *The Avengers of the New World: The Story of the Haitian Revolution* (Cambridge: Belknap Press of Harvard University Press, 2004).

11. Tensions flared up in Guadeloupe and Martinique; see Dubois, *Colony of Citizens*.

12. Garrigus, *Before Haiti*, especially 171–194.

13. Alex Dupuy, *Haiti in the World Economy: Class, Race, and Underdevelopment since 1700* (Boulder, Colo.: Westview, 1989), 44.

14. David Patrick Geggus, "The Bois Caïman Ceremony," in *Haitian Revolutionary Studies* (Bloomington: Indiana University Press, 2002), 81–96; Carolyn E. Fick, "The Saint Domingue Slave Insurrection of 1791: A Socio-Political and Cultural Analysis," *Journal of Caribbean History* 25 (1991): 1–40.

15. Madison Smartt Bell, *Toussaint Louverture: A Biography* (New York: Pantheon, 2007). For information on the rebels who remained loyal to the Spanish, see Jane G. Landers, *Atlantic Creoles in the Age of Revolution* (Cambridge: Harvard University Press, 2010).

16. "Letters of Toussaint Louverture and of Edward Stevens, 1798–1800," *American Historical Review* 16 (1910): 64–101.

17. David P. Geggus, "The Naming of Haiti," *New West Indian Guide* 71 (1997): 43–68.

18. David P. Geggus, ed., *Impact of the Haitian Revolution in the Atlantic World* (Columbia: University of South Carolina Press, 2001); David P. Geggus and Norman Fiering, eds., *The World of the Haitian Revolution* (Bloomington: Indiana University Press, 2009).

19. Black nationalism as understood by Haitians and Americans is discussed in chapter 5.

20. *Les Constitutions d'Haiti* (Paris: Louis-Joseph Janiver, 1886).

21. "African" had been the most common designation and continued to be used. James Sidbury, *Becoming African in America: Race and Nation in the Early Black Atlantic* (New York: Oxford University Press, 2007).

22. African Americans as a whole did not embrace racial notions of difference based on physical or biological characteristics, although increasingly some black individuals wrote of Africans' physical and moral superiority to whites in the later nineteenth century. Wilson Moses, *Afrotopia: The Roots of African American Popular History* (New York: Cambridge University Press, 1998), chaps. 2 and 3; Wilson Moses, *Golden Age of Black Nationalism, 1850–1925* (Hamden, Conn.: Archon, 1978).

23. Edward Bartlett Rugemer, "The Problem of Emancipation: The United States and Britain's Abolition of Slavery" (Ph.D. diss., Boston College, 2005); Steven Heath Mitton, "The Free World Confronted: The Problem of Slavery and Progress in American Foreign Relations, 1833–1844" (Ph.D. diss., Louisiana State University, 2005); Tim Matthewson, *A Proslavery Foreign Policy: Haitian-American Relations during the Early Republic* (Westport, Conn.: Praeger, 2003); Matthewson, "Jefferson and Haiti," *Journal of Southern History* 61 (1995): 209–248; Michael Zuckerman, "The Power of Blackness: Thomas Jefferson and the Revolution in St. Domingue," in *Almost Chosen People: Oblique Biographies in the American Grain* (Berkeley: University of California Press, 1993); Peter Onuf, *Jefferson's Empire: The Language of American Nationhood* (Charlottesville: University Press of Virginia, 2000); Donald R. Hickey, "America's Response to the Slave Revolt in Haiti, 1791–1806," *Journal of the Early Republic* 2 (1982): 361–379.

24. Benjamin Lundy, *A Plan for the Gradual Abolition of Slavery in the United States, without Danger or Loss to the Citizens of the South* (Baltimore: Benjamin Lundy, 1825); Robert Abzug, *Cosmos Crumbling: American Reform and Religious Imagination* (New York: Oxford University Press, 1994), 129–162; Gail Bederman, "Revisiting Nashoba: Slavery, Utopia, and Frances Wright in America, 1818–1826," *American Literary History* 17 (2005): 438–459.

25. By the 1830s, abolitionists in the United States abandoned this economic focus and adopted a new strategy of moral suasion under the leadership of William Garrison. In the British context, see Seymour Drescher, *The Mighty Experiment: Free Labor versus Slavery in British Emancipation* (Oxford: Oxford University Press, 2002).

26. Julie Winch, "American Free Blacks and Emigration to Haiti" (working paper 33, Centro de Investigaciones del Caribe y América Latina, Universidad Interamericana de Puerto Rico, San Germán, Puerto Rico, 1988); Alfred Hunt, *Haiti's Influence on Antebellum America: Slumbering Volcano in the Caribbean* (Baton Rouge: Louisiana State University Press, 1988), 168–172; James O. Jackson, "The Origins of Pan-African Nationalism: Afro-American and Haytian Relations, 1800–1863" (Ph.D. diss., Northwestern University, 1976), 78–117; Chris Dixon, *African America and Haiti: Emigration and Black Nationalism in the Nineteenth Century* (Westport, Conn.: Greenwood, 2000), Chapter 1.

Notes to Chapter 1

1. Mack Walker, *Germany and the Emigration, 1816-1885* (Cambridge: Harvard University Press, 1964), 38–41; Thomas H. Holloway, *Immigrants on the Land: Coffee and Society in Sao Paulo, 1886-1934* (Chapel Hill: University of North Carolina, 1980), 35–36. In Brazil during the 1870s, efforts were made to bring in immigrants to work as free workers on coffee plantations.

2. Robert P. Swierenga, *Faith and Family: Dutch Immigration and Settlement in the United States, 1820-1920* (New York: Holmes and Meier, 2000), xx.

3. The following Scholastic website creates interactive charts using data on immigration from 1820 to 2010: "Explore Immigration Data," http://teacher.scholastic.com/activities/immigration/immigration_data/index.htm.

4. For a brief overview of Ulster economic development, see Vivien Pollack, "Household Economy in Early Rural America and Ulster," in *Ulster and North America: Transatlantic Perspectives on the Scotch-Irish*, ed. Tyler Blethen and Curtis Wood, 61–75 (Tuscaloosa: University of Alabama Press, 1997).

5. Jim Webb, *Born Fighting: How the Scots-Irish Shaped America* (New York: Broadway Books, 2005).

6. Tyler H. Blethen and Curtis W. Wood, Jr., eds., *Ulster and North America: Transatlantic Perspectives on the Scotch-Irish* (Tuscaloosa: University of Alabama Press, 1997); Jonathan Bardon, *A History of Ulster* (Belfast: Blackstaff, 1992).

7. Kerby A. Miller, *Emigrants and Exiles: Ireland and the Irish Exodus to North America* (New York: Oxford University Press, 1985). This book remains the seminal work about Irish views of emigration as exile. See also Miller's more recent work *Irish Immigrants in the Land of Canaan: Letters and Memoirs from Colonial and Revolutionary America, 1675-1815* (New York: Oxford University Press, 2003).

8. Robert Kee, *The Green Flag*, 3 vols. (New York: Penguin Books, 1972).

9. Kerby Miller, "Irish Immigrants Who Perceive America as Exile," in *Major Problems in American Immigration and Ethnic History*, ed. Jon Gjerde, 113–122 (New York: Houghton Mifflin, 1998).

10. James M. Bergquist, *Daily Life in Immigrant America, 1820-1870* (Chicago: Ivan R. Dee, 2009).

11. Peter Way, *Common Labour and the Digging of North American Canals, 1780-1860* (New York: Cambridge University Press, 1993).

12. Maurice O'Connell, ed., *Daniel O'Connell: Political Pioneer* (Dublin: Institute of Public Administration, 1991).

13. Elizabeth Jane Errington, *Emigrant Worlds and Transatlantic Communities: Migration to Upper Canada in the First Half of the Nineteenth Century* (Montreal: McGill-Queens University Press, 2007), 16.

14. For the most in-depth overview of the American Colonization Society, see P. J. Staudenraus, *The African Colonization Movement, 1816-1865* (New York: Columbia University Press, 1961).

15. Walker, *Germany and the Emigration*, 7.

16. Ibid., chap. 1.

17. Ibid., 28.

18. Jeffrey Lesser, *Immigration, Ethnicity, and National Identity in Brazil, 1808 to the Present* (New York: Cambridge University Press, 2013).

19. Ibid., 31.

20. Robert A. Rockaway, *Words of the Uprooted: Jewish Immigrants in Early Twentieth-Century America* (Ithaca: Cornell University Press, 1998); Gary Dean Best, "Jacob H. Schiff's Galveston Movement: An Experiment in Immigration Deflection, 1907–1914," *American Jewish Archives* 30 (1978): 48.

Notes to Chapter 2

1. The French participated in the Atlantic slave trade until 1818, when they officially outlawed the trade. Unofficially, however, French slavers continued to sail the seas.

2. These leaders hoped to repeat what had occurred during the Haitian Revolution, with the Americans and British aligning against the French.

3. During Louverture's control of the island, he also attempted to reconcile the antislavery stand of the populace and the need for plantation crops worked by gang-like laborers.

4. Abraham Lincoln, message to Congress, December 1863, quoted in "Immigration Act (United States) (1864)," *Encyclopedia of Immigration*, February 16, 2011, http://immigration-online.org/145-immigration-act-united-states-1864.html.

5. "American Emigrant Company," *New York Times*, September 6, 1863.

6. Ibid.

7. Sam Schulman, "Juan Bautista Alberdi and His Influence on Immigration Policy in the Argentine Constitution of 1853," *Americas* 5 (1948): 3–17.

8. David Geggus, "The Naming of Haiti," *New West Indian Guide* 71 (1997): 43–68.

9. For the Haitian Revolution, see Laurent Dubois, *The Avengers of the New World: The Story of the Haitian Revolution* (Cambridge: Belknap Press of Harvard University Press, 2004).

10. John D. Garrigus, *Before Haiti: Race and Citizenship in French Saint-Domingue*, The Americas in the Early Modern Atlantic World (New York: Palgrave Macmillan, 2006), 303; Carolyn E. Fick, *The Making of Haiti: The Saint Domingue Revolution from Below* (Knoxville: University of Tennessee Press, 1990), 205.

11. Dubois, *Avengers of the New World*, 262–266.

12. The proclamation was reprinted in English-language publications such as the *Balance* (June 19, 1804, 197).

13. Women were left out of the equation altogether with Dessalines's constitution. The constitution expressly stated that all citizens must be "good fathers, good husbands and above all else, a good soldier . . . to be called a Haytien citizen." Quoted in Mimi Sheller, "Sword-Bearing Citizens: Militarism and Manhood in Nineteenth-Century Haiti," *Plantation Society in the Americas* 4 (1997): 244.

14. National identities throughout the eighteenth and nineteenth centuries had become increasingly predicated on color. Daniel K. Richter, *Facing East from Indian Country: A Native History of Early America* (Cambridge: Harvard

University Press, 2001); Peter Onuf, *Jefferson's Empire: The Language of American Nationhood* (Charlottesville: University Press of Virginia, 2000).

15. *Balance*, June 19, 1804, 197.

16. Alex Dupuy, *Haiti in the World Economy: Class, Race, and Underdevelopment since 1700* (Boulder, Colo.: Westview, 1989), 74.

17. James Graham Leyburn, *The Haitian People* (New Haven: Yale University Press, 1966), 36n. 4. On Dessalines and soldiers, see Carolyn Fick, "Emancipation in Haiti: From Plantation Labour to Peasant Proprietorship," *Slavery & Abolition* 21 (2000): 30.

18. Leyburn, *Haitian People*, 33–34.

19. Sheller, "Sword-Bearing Citizens," 260. All foreign observers commented on the commercial activities of Haitian women. As one observer noted, "Women . . . are free to follow any business they may choose, unrestricted by public opinion. They are bakers, coffee speculators, and coffee-housekeepers. They buy and sell most of the dry goods and much of the salt provisions which are imported." Benjamin Hunt, *Remarks on Hayti as a Place of Settlement for Afric-Americans; and on the Mulatto as a Race for the Tropic* (Philadelphia: T. B. Pugh, 1860), 9.

20. Dupuy, *Haiti in the World Economy*, 54 (sugar), 77 (coffee).

21. *Balance*, June 19, 1804, 197; *National Intelligencer*, April 6, 1804; Jonathan Brown, *History and Present Condition of St. Domingo* (Boston: Weeks, Jordan, 1839), 142; Sibylle Fischer, *Modernity Disavowed: Haiti and the Cultures of Slavery in the Age of Revolution* (Durham: Duke University Press, 2004), 240.

22. Jonathan Brown writes, "The first care which occupied the policy of Dessalines . . . was to repair the waste of population in the country from the long succession of war and massacre. For this purpose he refused to wait the slow operation of natural causes, but sought to attain his object by importation rather instead of reproduction" (*History and Present Condition*, 141).

23. Winthrop Jordan, *White over Black: American Attitudes towards the Negro, 1550–1812* (New York: Norton, 1968). Jordan discusses the reception of Jefferson's *Notes on the State of Virginia* (441). After Gabriel's Conspiracy was averted, Jefferson proposed transporting all ex-slaves to the island as the simplest solution to preventing a race war that manumission would unleash. Before 1804, when Dessalines declared Haitian independence, Jefferson believed America could contain the black revolutionaries. For a discussion of Jefferson, nation, and colonization, see Onuf, *Jefferson's Empire*, 147–188; Michael Zuckerman, "The Power of Blackness: Thomas Jefferson and the Revolution in St. Domingue," in *Almost Chosen People: Oblique Biographies in the American Grain* (Berkeley: University of California Press, 1993), 202; Donald R. Hickey, "America's Response to the Slave Revolt in Haiti, 1791–1806," *Journal of the Early Republic* 2 (1982): 365.

24. Thomas Jefferson, *Notes on the State of Virginia*, Query XIV, ed. William Peden (Chapel Hill: University of North Carolina Press, 1955), 138; Onuf, *Jefferson's Empire*, 150.

25. These massacres and Dessalines's refusal to allow the French residents to leave the country played directly into Jefferson's fundamental belief in the incompatibility of whites and their former slaves living together in one nation. It also reinforced the necessity of his diplomatic approach—to eliminate all contact

between the United States and Haiti. For more on Jefferson and his racial fears, see Zuckerman, "Power of Blackness."

26. Scholars who study Jefferson debate his true motive in destroying the relationship between the United States and Haiti. Some argue that the specter of large-scale slave resistance, like Gabriel's Conspiracy, brought home to Jefferson how dangerous the St. Domingue example could be to American slave masters. Tim Matthewson, "Jefferson and Haiti," *Journal of Southern History* 61 (1995): 227; Matthewson, "Jefferson and Nonrecognition of Haiti," *Proceedings of the American Philosophical Society* 140 (1996): 22. Matthewson's recent book also discusses the domestic influences working on Jefferson's foreign policy: *A Proslavery Foreign Policy: Haitian-American Relations during the Early Republic* (Westport, Conn.: Praeger, 2003). See also Onuf, *Jefferson's Empire*, chap. 5. Others believe that Jefferson's overriding ambition to secure Louisiana and Florida drove him to embrace Napoleon's friendship and to abandon Haiti. Douglas R. Egerton, "The Empire of Liberty Reconsidered," in *The Revolution of 1800: Democracy, Race, and the New Republic*, ed. James Horn, Jan Ellen Lewis, and Peter S. Onuf, 309–330 (Charlottesville: University of Virginia Press, 2002), 324; Hickey, "America's Response," 374; R. W. Logan, *The Diplomatic Relations of the United States with Haiti, 1776–1891* (New York: Kraus Reprint, 1969), 141–146; Donald L. Robinson, *Slavery in the Structure of American Politics, 1765–1820* (New York: Harcourt Brace Jovanovich, 1970), 368; Gordon S. Brown, *Toussaint's Clause: The Founding Fathers and the Haitian Revolution* (Jackson: University Press of Mississippi, 2005).

27. Dessalines's disdain for white people is demonstrated in this statement: "Hang a white man below one of the pans in the scales of the customs house, and put a sack of coffee in the other pan; the other whites will buy the coffee without paying attention to the body of their fellow whites." Beaubrun Ardouin, *Études sur l'histoire d'Haïti suivies de la vie du Général J.-M. Borgella*, 11 vols., 2nd ed. (Port-au-Prince: F. Dalencour, 1958), 6:26; David Nicholls, *From Dessalines to Duvalier: Race, Colour and National Independence in Haiti* (1979; repr., New York: Cambridge University Press, 1996), 37.

28. Ibid., 233.

29. Hickey, "America's Response," 365.

30. The embargo was passed one full year before the general embargo of 1806.

31. H. B. L. Hughes, "British Policy towards Haiti, 1801–1805," *Canadian Historical Review* 25 (1944): 397–408. Reviving trade relations with Dessalines provided the British with one way to recoup the enormous losses suffered in the ill-fated bid to conquer the island during the turmoil of the Haitian Revolution. David Geggus, *Slavery, War, and Revolution: The British Occupation of Saint-Domingue, 1793–1798* (New York: Oxford University Press, 1967). Although the British had much to fear—their largest colony in the Caribbean, Jamaica, was Haiti's close neighbor—they believed any potential threat from the island nation could be contained easily by British sea power. The attempted conquest ended in complete disaster, with thirty thousand lives lost, and the British treasury was estimated to have spent £40 million on the expedition.

32. *National Intelligencer*, November 21, 1804.

33. For the most comprehensive study of Dessalines in power, see Leyburn, *Haitian People*, 32–42.

34. Nicholls, *From Dessalines to Duvalier*, 48.

35. Logan, *Diplomatic Relations*, 183–185.

36. During the colonial period, slaves cultivated plots of land to supplement food supplies. See Sidney W. Mintz, "Slavery and the Rise of Peasantries," *Historical Reflections / Reflexions Historiques* 6 (1979): 213–242. St. Domingue planters still relied on imports for much of their slaves' food, including flour, salt, rice, codfish, and dried salted beef. See Dupuy, *Haiti in the World Economy*, 40–43.

37. An online version of the extremely rare document "Code Henry" can be accessed at the Internet Archive, Boston Public Library, http://www.archive.org/details/codehenryoohait (accessed May 16, 2011).

38. Leyburn, *Haitian People*, 44–45.

39. "No. 18, Mackenzie to the Earl of Dudley" (extract), London, March 31, 1828, in *British and Foreign State Papers, 1828–1829*, 2 vols. (London, 1831), 2:702.

40. Christophe also replaced his coinage with gold and silver coins, adding to the idea of the wealth of the kingdom. "No. 3, Mr. Consul-General Mackenzie to Mr. Secretary Canning" (extract), Port-au-Prince, September 9, 1826, in *British and Foreign State Papers*, 2:667.

41. "Bank of England," *Niles' Weekly Register*, June 13, 1818. In 1820, the king's treasury possessed a $6 million reserve. "No. 3, Mackenzie to Canning," 2:667.

42. Robert K. LaCerte, "Evolution of Land and Labour in the Haitian Revolution, 1791–1820," in *Caribbean Freedom: Society and Economy from Emancipation to the Present*, ed. Hilary Beckles and Verene Shepard, 42–47 (London: Currey, 1993), 45.

43. Leyburn, *Haitian People*, 61.

44. From Pétion's perspective, taxing coffee heavily put money into the treasury.

45. On the early move to coffee within St. Domingue, see Michel-Rolph Trouillot, "The Inconvenience of Freedom: Free People of Color and the Political Aftermath of Slavery in Dominica and Saint-Domingue/Haiti," in *The Meanings of Freedom: The Economics, Politics, and Culture after Slavery*, ed. Frank McGlynn and Seymour Drescher, 147–182 (Pittsburgh: University of Pittsburgh Press, 1992).

46. To avoid this scenario for the future, Pétion could have cut the standing army. But he needed this army to protect the republic from the continuing menace of France.

47. *Times*, November 27, 1807; Herbert Cole, *Christophe, King of Haiti* (New York: Viking, 1967), 160.

48. Karen Racine, "Britannia's Bold Brother: British Cultural Influence in Haiti during the Reign of Henry Christophe," *Journal of Caribbean History* 33 (1999): 128.

49. *Henry Christophe and Thomas Clarkson: A Correspondence*, ed. Earl Leslie Griggs and Clifford H. Prator, 38–62 (New York: Greenwood, 1968), 57–59; David Geggus, "Haiti and the Abolitionists: Opinion, Propaganda and International Politics in Britain and France, 1804–1838," in *Abolition and Its Aftermath: The Historical Context, 1790–1916*, ed. David Richardson, 113–140 (London: Frank Cass, 1985).

50. Planters and shippers who were part of the so-called Ultra-Royalists party continued to push for military reconquest of the island until 1825.

51. Nicholls, *From Dessalines to Duvalier*, 47–51.

52. Boyer learned from his predecessors' frustrations, and the next chapter includes a discussion of Boyer's efforts to gain recognition.

53. "Henri I," *Atheneum*, May 1, 1821, 98; Racine, "Britannia's Bold Brother," 133.

54. One publication estimated that his army consisted of fifty thousand men. *Analetic Magazine*, May 1817, 406. Evidence suggests that workers regularly fled the kingdom's harsh labor conditions for the republic.

55. Christophe to Clarkson, April 26, 1818, in Griggs and Prator, *Henry Christophe and Thomas Clarkson*, 108–109.

56. Ibid.

57. Baron de Vastey to Clarkson, November 29, 1819, in ibid., 180.

58. Nicholls, *From Dessalines to Duvalier*, 53. When Christophe claimed the northern region of Haiti, he wrote up his own constitution, leaving out this aspect of Dessalines's constitution. It was only at the insistence of Thomas Clarkson that Christophe limited landownership to white people in towns and ports.

59. *Niles' Weekly Register*, October 28, 1820. Ada Ferrer has uncovered evidence in the Spanish and Cuban archives that shows that both Christophe and Pétion were known among Cubans to be interested in freeing slaves and in bringing former St. Domingue refugees back to Haiti. See Ferrer, "Speaking of Haiti: Slavery, Revolution, and Freedom in Cuban Slave Testimony," in *The World of the Haitian Revolution*, ed. David Patrick Geggus and Norman Fiering, 223–247 (Bloomington: Indiana University Press, 2009).

60. Clarkson to Christophe, June 28, 1819, in Griggs and Prator, *Henry Christophe and Thomas Clarkson*, 142 (English language); Clarkson to Christophe, September 28, 1819, in ibid., 162 ("dollars!").

61. Prince Saunders had been sent to Haiti by the African Institute in the 1810s as an educational consultant. Arthur O. White, "Prince Saunders: An Instance of Social Mobility among Antebellum New England Blacks," *Journal of Negro History* 60 (1975): 526–535.

62. The London publication of 1816 includes the chapter "Reflections of the Editor," which was deleted for the Boston edition. The chapter praises Christophe and castigates Pétion as a traitor to the Haitian people since he had "renounced real independence," referring to the rumor of his negotiations with France. *Haytian Papers: A Collection of the Very Interesting Proclamations, and Other Official Documents; Together with Some Account of the Rise, Progress, and Present State of the Kingdom of Hayti* (1816; repr., Boston: Caleb Bingham, 1818), 192–193.

63. Prince Saunders, *Address Delivered at Bethel Church, Philadelphia; on the 30th of September, 1818: Before the Pennsylvania Augustine Society, for the Education of People of Colour* (Philadelphia: Joseph Rakestraw, 1818); Saunders, *A Memoir Presented to the American Convention for Promoting the Abolition of Slavery, and Improving the Condition of the African Race, December 11th, 1818* (Philadelphia: Dennis Heartt, 1818).

64. An in-depth discussion of Christophe's kingdom can be found in Sybille Fischer, *Modernity Disavowed: Haiti and the Cultures of Slavery in the Age of Revolution* (Durham: Duke University Press, 2004).

65. Cole, *Christophe, King of Haiti*; Michel-Rolph Trouillot, *Silencing the Past: Power and the Production of History* (Boston: Beacon, 1995).

66. *Republican Watchtower*, May 19, 1807.

67. James Tredwell, a member of the New York African American community, traveled to the republic in 1816 to investigate conditions on the island. Upon his return, Tredwell published information on the settlement project in 1817: *The Constitution of the Republic of Hayti; to Which Is Added Documents Relating to the Correspondence of His Most Christian Majesty, with the President of Hayti; Preceded by a Proclamation to the People and the Army* (New York: James Tredwell, 1818), 7.

68. Ibid., 5-6.

69. Ibid., 7.

70. Ibid.

71. Notary record in Port-au-Plat: José Augusto Puig Ortiz, *Emigración de libertos norteamericans a Puerto Plata en la primera mitad del siglo XIX: La Iglesia Metodista Wesleyana* (Santo Domingo: Alfa y Omega, 1978), 98-99. The record states that Tredwell had been living there for ten years in 1827.

72. John Edward Baur, "Mulatto Machiavelli, Jean Pierre Boyer, and the Haiti of His Day," *Journal of Negro History* 32 (1947): 307-353.

73. Ibid., 309-310.

74. *Niles' Weekly Register*, October 17, 1818; and *National Messenger*, June 26, 1820.

75. *National Gazette*, March 24, 1821.

76. *Niles' Weekly Register*, February 17, 1821. *Niles' Weekly Register* and *National Gazette and Literary Register* both published information about Boyer's initial emigration offer.

77. *National Messenger*, June 26, 1820.

78. *Niles' Weekly Register*, July 1, 1820.

79. A Baltimore Haytian Society was formed among free blacks, but whether they traveled to Haiti remains unknown. *Niles' Weekly Register*, February 17, 1821. John Griffith, a public porter, left Philadelphia in 1819 for the republic to settle "there permanently." Michael Nash, "Research Note: Searching for Working-Class Philadelphia in the Records of the Philadelphia Saving Fund Society," *Journal of Social History* 29 (1996): 684.

Notes to Chapter 3

1. Robert K. LaCerte, "Xenophobia and Economic Decline: The Haitian Case, 1820-1843," *Americas* 37 (1981): 508.

2. Countries in Latin America received diplomatic recognition from France, Great Britain, or the United States.

3. Gregory Weeks, "Almost Jeffersonian: U.S. Recognition Policy toward Latin America," *Presidential Studies Quarterly* 31 (2001): 492.

4. Boyer did continue to negotiate with French authorities during this time as well.

5. Michel-Rolph Trouillot, *Haiti, State against Nation: The Origins and Legacy of Duvalierism* (New York: Monthly Review Press, 1990), 52–53; Michael Zuckerman, "The Power of Blackness: Thomas Jefferson and the Revolution in St. Domingue," in *Almost Chosen People: Oblique Biographies in the American Grain* (Berkeley: University of California Press, 1993), 176; Donald R. Hickey, "America's Response to the Slave Revolt in Haiti, 1791–1806," *Journal of the Early Republic* 2 (1982): 378.

6. *Niles' Weekly Register*, June 10, 1820.

7. *Niles' Weekly Register*, February 10, 1821.

8. *Newburyport Herald*, March 6, 1821.

9. *Newburyport Gazette*, February 19, 1822.

10. *National Gazette*, January 19, 1822.

11. *Le Propagateur*, vol. 3, 1822.

12. *Poulson's American Daily Advertiser*, February 24, 1823; *Le Propagateur*, vol. 3, 1822.

13. *Niles' Weekly Register*, November 11, 1820.

14. *Niles' Weekly Register*, September 27, 1823.

15. *Niles' Weekly Register*, February 9, 1822.

16. *National Gazette*, April 17, 1822.

17. *Boston Patriot*, July 16, 1823.

18. *Niles' Weekly Register*, September 7, 1822.

19. These events included the embargo of 1806, the War of 1812 or the Second War of Independence, the Napoleonic Wars in Europe, and the Spanish American wars of independence.

20. For a thorough review of American economic growth after the American Revolution, see Douglass C. North, *The Economic Growth of the United States, 1790–1860* (Englewood Cliffs, N.J.: Prentice Hall, 1961). For American-Haitian economic and political policies, through 1804, see Gordon S. Brown, *Toussaint's Clause: The Founding Fathers and the Haitian Revolution* (Jackson: University Press of Mississippi, 2005).

21. In British Parliament, Lord Broughman explained that it was "well worthwhile to incur a loss . . . in order, by the glut, to stifle in the cradle those rising in manufactures in the United States." *Niles' Weekly Register*, December 1816; Norris W. Preyer, "Southern Support of the Tariff of 1816—A Reappraisal," *Journal of Southern History* 25 (1959): 312.

22. R. W. Logan, *Diplomatic Relations of the United States with Haiti, 1776–1891* (New York: Kraus Reprint, 1969), 194.

23. The Panic was started by a contraction in the banking sector as well as a sudden drop in demand from Europe. For the only book-length study of the Panic, see Murray N. Rothbard, *The Panic of 1819: Reactions and Policies* (New York: Columbia University Press, 1962).

24. By 1820, a barrel of flour cost four dollars, almost a third of its 1817 value. Mary H. W. Hargreaves, *The Presidency of John Quincy Adams* (Lawrence: University Press of Kansas, 1985), 12.

25. Mathew Carey, "Address to the Farmers of the United States," *Essays in Political Economy* (Philadelphia, 1822), 419; Samuel Rezneck, "Depression of 1819–1822: A Social History," *American Historical Review* 39 (1933): 30.

26. Logan, *Diplomatic Relations*, 194.

27. American manufacturers, hit by the resumption of peace in Europe and by increased British competition, were working at 50 percent of their pre-1815 capacity. David J. Lehman, "Explaining Hard Times: Political Economy and the Panic of 1819 in Philadelphia" (Ph.D. diss., University of California–Los Angeles, 1992), 179.

28. *National Intelligencer*, reprinted in *Genius of Universal Emancipation*, December 1821. The article mentioned that "nine thousand barrels of flour, one thousand and fifty tierces of rice, five hundred and thirty-three barrels of port, [and] thirty-two thousand hams" had been sold; 33,123 barrels of flour were sold in Port-au-Prince in 1825 (*Niles' Weekly Register*, July 16, 1825).

29. *Niles' Weekly Register*, March 23, 1822.

30. *Niles' Weekly Register*, September 7, 1822.

31. *Boston Patriot*, September 7, 1822.

32. *Boston Patriot*, July 16, 1823; *Poulson's American Daily Advertiser*, January 24 and January 29, 1823; *Newburyport Herald*, August 16, 1822.

33. *Baltimore Patriot*, March 29, 1815.

34. Complaints about this disparity were widespread in newspapers. *National Gazette*, March 31, April 11, and August 25, 1821; *Essex Register*, April 4, 1821.

35. The *Boston Centinel* writer had been quoted in the *National Gazette*, March 31, 1821.

36. *Poulson's American Daily Advertiser*, January 24, 1823.

37. *United States Gazette*, February 26, 1824.

38. Quoted in Jackson, "Origins of Pan-African Nationalism: Afro-American and Haytian Relations, 1800–1863" (Ph.D. diss., Northwestern University, 1976), 41.

39. *Baltimore Patriot*, September 8, 1821.

40. Rothbard, *Panic of 1819*, v. Rothbard notes that newspaper editors were some of the "leading economists of the day."

41. *Niles' Weekly Register*, April 12, 1823.

42. In Baltimore, the price of a barrel of flour dropped every year between 1815 and 1820. Wheat had become increasingly important to the economies of the middle southern states of Virginia, Maryland, and North Carolina in the 1800s. See Clyde Haulman, "Virginia Commodity Prices during the Panic of 1819," *Journal of the Early Republic* 22 (2002): 675–688.

43. For Baltimore's development as a wheat port, see Geoffrey N. Gilbert, "Baltimore's Flour Trade to the Caribbean, 1750–1815," *Journal of Economic History* 37 (1977): 249–251; and Pearle Blood, "Factors in the Economic Development of Baltimore, Maryland," *Economic Geography* 13 (1937): 187–208.

44. *National Gazette*, December 6, 1825. This repayment also raised Haiti's credit rating, which, according to one source, had been "somewhat impaired." These policies were expensive for Haiti. Though Boyer received a boon when gold from Christophe's treasury was sent to Port-au-Prince, by 1822, the treasury was once again in debt (Trouillot, *Haiti, State against Nation*, 49). British consul Charles Mackenzie wrote that it was worth $6 million. "No. 3, Mr. Consul-General Mackenzie to Mr. Secretary Canning" (extract), Port-au-Prince,

September 9, 1826, in *British and Foreign State Papers, 1828–1829*, 2 vols. (London, 1831), 2:667.

45. W. Jeffrey Bolster, *Black Jacks: African American Seamen in the Age of Sail* (Cambridge: Harvard University Press, 1997), 147–148.

46. Andrew Armstrong to Secretary of State Henry Clay, June 14, 1825, U.S. State Department Consular Despatches, Cape Haitien Series, vol. 4: "On several occasions when the case has been absolutely a flagrant injustice, the President has discountenanced the practice." Unfortunately, I have not found any such cases in my research.

47. *Newburyport Gazette*, October 19, 1821.

48. *Poulson's American Daily Advertiser*, February 24, 1823; *Le Propagateur*, vol. 3, 1822.

49. *Niles' Weekly Register*, September 16, 1820; *Bangor Weekly Register*, September 21, 1820.

50. See letters in *Haitian Papers, 1811–1846: Comprising Proclamations, Decrees, Occasional Numbers of Official Gazettes*, Rare Book Division, New York Public Library, 34–37. These include a letter from Robert Golden, John Milroy, and J. R. Bernard to Boyer, dated August 18, 1820, stating that the fire was deliberately set, as more fires were started during the subsequent days (37), and a second letter, dated August 18, 1820, from sixteen foreign merchants (34). The merchants wanted to publish their own report, but this report was suppressed by Boyer, who refused to grant approval for its printing. "Proposed Letter to the President," in ibid., 38.

51. For patent taxes on merchants, see No. 946, "Loi sur les patentes," Port-au-Prince, April 19, 1825, in Baron S. Linstant, *Recueil général des lois et actes du gouvernement d'Haïti, depuis la proclamation de son indépendance jusqu'à nos jours*, 5 vols. (Paris: Auguste Durand, 1851–1860), 4:174; for duties on building supplies, see *Niles' Weekly Register*, September 16, 1820. Boyer increasingly relied on money lent by foreign merchants to meet Haiti's debt payments. Trouillot, *Haiti, State against Nation*, 68–69.

52. *Newburyport Gazette*, January 17, 1823 ("incendiary"); *Poulson's American Daily Advertiser*, January 16, 1823 (losses). For detailed reports on the fire, see *Poulson's American Daily Advertiser*, January 25, 1823. *Le Telegraphe* reported that the 1822 fire was "more afflicting" than that of 1820. *Le Telegraphe*, December 19, 1822; *Poulson's American Daily Advertiser*, January 14, 1823.

53. Mimi Sheller, *Democracy after Slavery: Black Publics and Peasant Radicalism in Haiti and Jamaica* (New York: Macmillan, 2000), 114; David Nicholls, *From Dessalines to Duvalier: Race, Colour and National Independence in Haiti* (1979; repr., New York: Cambridge University Press, 1996), 72.

54. *Le Telegraphe*, September 1, 1822; *National Gazette*, September 28, 1822.

55. *Newburyport Gazette*, October 4, 1822.

56. *Connecticut Journal*, October 8, 1822; *Boston Commercial Gazette*, October 10, 1822. These papers translated the official Haitian report released by Boyer without any additional commentary

57. *Genius of Universal Emancipation*, December 1822.

58. Ibid.

59. *Boston Centinel*, August 10, 1822.

60. *Newburyport Herald*, March 19, 1822. The *Alexandria Herald*, May 12, 1822, reported that Boyer's private secretary was on his way to England to petition for British acknowledgment of Haitian independence.

61. *Poulson's American Daily Advertiser*, January 29, 1823.

62. *United States Gazette*, February 16, 1824.

63. Quoted in Logan, *Diplomatic Relations*, 198.

64. *Newburyport Herald*, August 16, 1822; *Niles' Weekly Register*, August 17, 1822; *Boston Centinel*, August 10, 1822. All three of these newspapers reported on Boyer's letter.

65. *Genius of Universal Emancipation*, December 1822.

66. *Poulson's American Daily Advertiser*, January 29, 1823. Howard might be the same writer who wrote a series of essays during the years of the Panic of 1819 on the U.S. economy (Samuel Rezneck, "Depression of 1819–1822," 35). Rothbard also cites the use of "Howard" by Mordecai Manuel Noah, the publisher of the *National Advocate* (*Panic of 1819*, 33).

67. *Boston Patriot*, September 7, 1822.

68. Unfortunately, most of the entries for 1822 and 1823 are missing from the diary of John Quincy Adams. John Quincy Adams, *Memoirs of John Quincy Adams, Comprising Portions of His Diary from 1795–1848*, ed. Charles Francis Adams, 12 vols. (Philadelphia: Lippincott, 1874–1877).

69. *National Gazette*, January 22, 1824.

70. Michael P. Johnson, "Denmark Vesey and His Co-Conspirators," *William and Mary Quarterly*, 3rd ser., 58 (2001): 965n. 184. In Johnson's reappraisal of the conspiracy, he discusses why Vesey and his fellow black Charlestonians would have evoked Boyer and how Haiti would have served as a potential refuge. He concludes that the subject of Haiti had appeared several times in the *Charleston Courier*. Richard C. Wade first questioned how "real" the Denmark Vesey Conspiracy was in "The Vesey Plot: A Reconsideration," *Journal of Southern History* 30 (1964): 143–161; and in his book *Slavery in the Cities: The South, 1820–1860* (New York: Oxford University Press, 1967).

71. *National Intelligencer*, August 19, 1822.

72. *Boston Patriot*, September 7, 1822; *Boston Commercial Gazette*, August 29, 1822.

73. Boyer wrote letters to private individuals such as John Dodge of Massachusetts. *Newburyport Gazette*, August 16, 1822; *Niles' Weekly Register*, August 17, 1822; *Southern Chronicle* (Camden, S.C.), September 11, 1822.

74. *Boston Patriot*, September 7, 1822.

75. *Niles' Weekly Register*, September 27, 1823.

76. Martinique: *Niles' Weekly Register*, February 14, 1824; Jamaica: *United States Gazette*, November 25, 1823.

77. *United States Gazette*, February 16, 1824. The proclamation was dated January 6, 1824. Proclamation 873, "Proclamation du Président d'Haiti pour l'organisation des gardes nationales," in Linstant, *Recueil*, 4:2–3.

78. The authorities in South Carolina passed laws to prevent contact between sailors and slaves in what were called Negro Seaman Acts, which required all black sailors to spend the duration of the ship's time in port

in jail. They also required the sailors to pay the expenses incurred while incarcerated.

79. *Poulson's American Daily Advertiser*, May 23, 1823.

80. Ibid.

81. British policy toward American trade in the Caribbean also underwent a change in 1822 that lessened the need for Haitian trade. The British relaxed their prohibition of American trade in some of their colonial ports.

82. *Le Propagateur*, February 18, 1824; *United States Gazette*, February 25, 1824; *New York Gazette*, February 23, 1824; *Le Propagateur*, June 6, 1824; *United States Gazette*, August 5, 1824.

83. Many members of the American Colonization Society, a society that proposed sending freed slaves to its colony on the west coast of Africa, were southerners. For a picture of the southern abolitionist movement, see James Brewer Stewart, "Evangelicalism and the Radical Strain in Southern Antislavery Thought during the 1820s," *Journal of Southern History* 39 (1973): 379–396; Eric Burin, *Slavery and the Peculiar Solution: A History of the American Colonization Society* (Gainesville: University Press of Florida, 2005); Marie Tyler-McGraw, "Richmond Free Blacks and African Colonization, 1816–1832," *Journal of American Studies* 21, no. 2 (1987): 207–224.

84. *Le Telegraphe*, July 25, 1824, reprinted in *Niles' Weekly Register*, September 11, 1824.

85. For the whitening of America, see William W. Freehling, *Reintegration of American History: Slavery and the Civil War* (New York: Oxford University Press, 1994).

86. *Le Telegraphe*, July 25, 1824.

87. Ibid.

88. William W. Freehling, *The Road to Disunion: Secessionists at Bay, 1776–1854* (New York: Oxford University Press, 1990); Freehling, *Reintegration of American History*.

Notes to Chapter 4

1. The classic work on the ACS continues to be P. J. Staudenraus, *The African Colonization Movement, 1816–1865* (New York: Columbia University Press, 1961). For more recent works, see Eric Burin, *Slavery and the Peculiar Solution: A History of the American Colonization Society* (Gainesville: University Press of Florida, 2005); Claude A. Clegg, *Price of Liberty: African Americans and the Making of Liberia* (Chapel Hill: University North Carolina Press, 2004). Later in the nineteenth century for other New World nations, the solution to the whitening of the population was to open and encourage migration from Europe. See Richard Graham, ed., *The Idea of Race in Latin America: 1870–1940* (Austin: University of Texas Press, 1990).

2. Elizabeth Jane Errington, *Emigrant Worlds and Transatlantic Communities: Migration to Upper Canada in the First Half of the Nineteenth Century* (Montreal: McGill-Queen's University Press, 2007), 19.

3. Mack Walker, *Germany and the Emigration, 1816–1885* (Cambridge: Harvard University Press, 1964), 60.

4. Errington, *Emigrant Worlds*, 17.

5. Bernard Bailyn argues, in *Voyages to the West: A Passage of the Peopling of America on the Eve of the Revolution* (New York: Knopf, 1986), that this "new" migration was nothing new but merely an extension of the eighteenth-century movements that had halted as a result of the wars and revolutions of the Napoleonic era.

6. Errington, *Emigrant Worlds*, 16.

7. For documents relating to this migration, see "Projects," Peannairi web forum, http://peannairi.com/texts/. For a recent book on some of these land-settlement groups, see Robert C. Lee, *Canada Company and the Huron Tract, 1826–1853: Personalities, Profits and Politics* (Toronto: Natural History, 2004). Wilmot-Horton also published a book of correspondence that gives details about the transportation, settlement, and financing of the plan: Sir Robert Wilmot-Horton and A. C. Buchanan, *Emigration Practically Considered* (London: Henry Colburn, 1828).

8. Wilmot-Horton's ideas did influence future reformers and played a part in the Australian scheme to use the sale of land in Australia to fund emigration. See "Horton, Sir Robert Wilmot (1784–1841)," *Australian Dictionary of Biography*, National Centre of Biography, Australian National University, http://adb.anu.edu.au/biography/horton-sir-robert-wilmot-2199/text2841 (accessed July 3, 2013).

9. In addition to the excellent book by Elizabeth Jane Errington, *Emigrant Worlds*, two other recent studies of this group are Wendy Cameron, Sheila Haines, and Mary McDougall Maude, eds., *English Immigrant Voices: Labourers' Letters from Upper Canada in the 1830s* (Montreal: McGill-Queens University Press, 2000); and Wendy Cameron and Mary McDougall Maude, eds., *Assisting Emigration to Upper Canada: The Petworth Project, 1832–1837* (Montreal: McGill-Queens University Press, 2000).

10. William Freehling, *The Road to Disunion* (New York: Oxford University Press, 1990), 159–160.

11. There are a few biographies of Lundy and Niles. None exist for Dewey. For Niles, see William Kovarik, "To Avoid the Coming Storm: Hezekiah Niles' *Weekly Register* as a Voice of North-South Moderation, 1811–1836," *American Journalism*, Summer 1992; Norval Neil Luxon, *"Niles' Weekly Register": News Magazine of the Nineteenth Century* (Baton Rouge: Louisiana State University Press, 1947); Richard G. Stone, *Hezekiah Niles as an Economist* (Baltimore: Johns Hopkins University Press, 1933). For Lundy, see Merton L. Dillon, *Benjamin Lundy and the Struggle for Negro Freedom* (Urbana: University of Illinois Press, 1966); Thomas Earle, ed., *The Life, Travels and Opinions of Benjamin Lundy, 1789–1839* (1847; repr., New York: A. M. Kelley, 1971).

12. Stone, *Hezekiah Niles as an Economist*.

13. Even before the formation of the ACS, Lundy had recommended deportation schemes as part of emancipation when he was a member of the Union Humane Society of Ohio. See Henry N. Sherwood, "Formation of the American Colonization Society," *Journal of Negro History* (1917): 211.

14. William Lloyd Garrison, quoted in Robert Abzug, *Cosmos Crumbling: American Reform and Religious Imagination* (New York: Oxford University Press, 1994), 141.

15. Niles began urging this in his *Niles' Weekly Register* article of July 3, 1824.

16. *National Advocate*, June 23, 1824.

17. Jefferson returned to this idea in 1824 (Freehling, *Road to Disunion*, 156).

18. For discussion of Jefferson and his fears, see Peter Onuf, *Jefferson's Empire: The Language of American Nationhood* (Charlottesville: University Press of Virginia, 2000), chap. 5; Tim Matthewson, "Jefferson and Haiti," *Journal of Southern History* 61 (1995): 209–248; Matthewson, *Proslavery Foreign Policy: Haitian-American Relations during the Early Republic* (New York: Praeger, 2003); Michael Zuckerman, "The Power of Blackness: Thomas Jefferson and the Revolution in St. Domingue," in *Almost Chosen People: Oblique Biographies in the American Grain* (Berkeley: University of California Press, 1993).

19. Christopher Phillips, *Freedom's Port: The African American Community of Baltimore, 1790–1860* (Urbana: University of Illinois Press, 1997), 15, table 1 (population numbers for Baltimore City).

20. Population numbers for New York City derive from Leslie M. Harris, *In the Shadow of Slavery: African Americans in New York City, 1626–1863* (Chicago: University of Chicago Press, 2003), 117.

21. For Philadelphia population figures, see Gary Nash, *Forging Freedom: The Formation of Philadelphia's Black Community, 1720–1840* (Cambridge: Harvard University Press, 1988), 137, table 4; for percentage of population in 1820, see Leonard P. Curry, *The Free Black in Urban America, 1800–1850* (Chicago: University of Chicago Press, 1981), 246, appendix A, table 1-2.

22. Finley wrote *Thoughts on the Colonization of Free Blacks* (Washington, D.C., 1816) to gather support for the idea of the "separation of the black from the white population" (1) and argued that Africa was the best place for such a colony of blacks, as it was the "country of their fathers" (7). Douglas Egerton, in "'Its Origin Is Not a Little Curios': A New Look at the American Colonization Society," *Journal of the Early Republic* 5 (1985): 463–480, unveils evidence that rather than Finley being the founding figure of the society, Mercer deserves to be given full credit for establishing the American Colonization Society (because he came to the idea earlier than Finley did).

23. State auxiliary societies could be found in Connecticut, Kentucky, Louisiana, Maryland, Massachusetts, Mississippi, New Jersey, New York, Ohio, Pennsylvania, Vermont, and Virginia.

24. American Society for Colonizing the Free People of Colour of the United States, *The Eleventh Annual Report of the American Society for Colonizing the Free People of Colour of the United States* (Washington, D.C.: James C. Dunn, 1828), 18.

25. *National Recorder*, November 20, 1820.

26. *Poulson's American Daily Advertiser*, February 13, 1819.

27. Staudenraus, *Colonization Society*, 33.

28. Julie Winch, *A Gentleman of Color: The Life of James Forten* (New York: Oxford University Press, 2002), 191.

29. Marie Tyler-McGraw argues, in "Richmond Free Blacks and African Colonization," *Journal of American Studies* 21, no. 2 (1987): 207–224, that in Richmond, free blacks did support the ACS's Liberian colony and that one hundred of that city's black population settled there in the 1820s.

30. *National Recorder*, November 20, 1820.

31. *Boston Recorder*, May 15, 1824; Burin states that between 1820 and 1830, 29 percent of the colony's population died. Burin, *Slavery and the Peculiar Solution*, 17.

32. Staudenraus, *Colonization Society*, 89, 269n18.

33. In 1822, rather than send free blacks to the ACS colony at Mesurado, the Baltimore Colonization Society chose to begin its own colony near the Pongo River. See Bruce L. Mouser, "Baltimore's African Experiment, 1822–1827," *Journal of Negro History* 80 (1995): 113–130.

34. Michael J. Turner, "The Limits of Abolition: Government, Saints, and the 'African Question,'" *English Historical Review* 112 (1997): 319–357.

35. *New York American*, June 18, 1824.

36. Staudenraus, *Colonization Society*, 81 (fund raising), 76 ("crisis").

37. The ACS had from its inception envisioned working in partnership with the federal government, and it had petitioned Washington several times for direct financial assistance. The government rebuffed these requests.

38. *Genius of Universal Emancipation*, February 1825.

39. *Niles' Weekly Register*, June 26, 1824.

40. Staudenraus, *Colonization Society*, 77–78.

41. *Genius of Universal Emancipation*, January 1822.

42. *Niles' Weekly Register*, July 3, 1824.

43. Ibid.

44. *New York American*, July 23, 1824.

45. Jonathas Henri Théodore Granville, *Biographie de Jonathas Granville par son fils* (Paris: E. Brière, 1873), 120–122; *New York Commercial Advertiser*, June 21, 1824.

46. Lundy couched emigration in these terms—of wanting a white America—knowing that this would add to its appeal. Lundy has received a full-length biography that discusses his attitude toward black America: Dillon, *Benjamin Lundy*.

47. *National Advocate*, July 20, 1824. Boyer's appeals had hit their intended mark.

48. *Niles' Weekly Register*, June 26, 1824.

49. Ruth Nuermberger, *The Free Produce Movement: A Quaker Protest against Slavery* (Durham: Duke University Press, 1942). More recent studies of this movement include Lawrence B. Glickman, *Buying Power: A History of Consumer Activism* (Chicago: University of Chicago Press, 2009); and Carol Faulkner, "The Root of the Evil: Free Produce and Radical Antislavery, 1820–1860," *Journal of the Early Republic* 27 (2007): 377–405.

50. French Guyana, a French colony in South America, was being established as free labor colony at this time. France advertised settlement opportunities to free African Americans. See *United States Gazette*, June 10, 1824; *Niles' Weekly Register*, September 11, 1824; Granville, *Biographie*, 126; *National Gazette*, June 22, 1824.

51. The practice crossed the Atlantic and found a voice in the writings of Thomas Branagan, specifically in his "Buying Stolen Goods Synonymous with Stealing," in

The Penitential Tyrant; or, Slave Trader Reformed: A Patriotic Poem in Four Cantos (New York: Samuel Wood, 1807).

52. Advocates for free labor and free produce were also making their voices heard in England in the 1820s. James Cropper and Elizabeth Heyrick were both abolitionists who proposed some form of free labor and free produce to defeat slavery. For a comparison of their two perspectives, see David Brion Davis, "James Cropper and the British Anti-Slavery Movement, 1823–1833," *Journal of Negro History* 45 (1961): 155–156.

53. There were some Quakers involved in the free produce movement who were not directly associated with Haitian emigration. Quaker merchant Jeremiah Thompson also advertised his preference for free labor products. Thompson, famous for his development of the Black Ball Line of packet ships between New York and Liverpool, was a cotton baron who made his fortune in the cotton trade. According to Lundy, Thompson showed a preference for buying cotton from free laborers. See *Genius of Universal Emancipation*, September 17, 1825.

54. Elias Hicks, *Letters of Elias Hicks: Including Also Observations on the Slavery of the Africans and Their Descendants, and on the Use of the Produce of their Labor* (Philadelphia, 1861).

55. *United States Gazette*, December 25, 1824.

56. Nuermberger, *Free Produce Movement*, appendix.

57. *Niles' Weekly Register*, June 25, 1824.

58. Loring Dewey, *Correspondence Relative to the Emigration to Hayti, of the Free People of Colour, in the United States; Together with the Instructions to the Agent Sent Out by President Boyer* (New York: Mahlon Day, 1824), 15.

59. For a discussion of Lundy's free labor advocacy and its effect on his antislavery activism, see Dillon, *Benjamin Lundy*, 76–78.

60. *Genius of Universal Emancipation*, December 1824.

61. Nuermberger, *Free Produce Movement*, 21.

62. As samples of the intense interest in Granville, see *United States Gazette*, June 21, 1824; *Poulson's American Daily Advertiser*, July 13, 1824; *Niles' Weekly Register*, July 3, 1824; *National Gazette*, June 29, 1824; *Commercial Courant*, June 29, 1824; *National Advocate*, June 29, 1824; *Genius of Universal Emancipation*, November 1824; *Cincinnati Literary Gazette*, July 17, 1824; *Connecticut Courant*, June 29, 1824; *New York Observer*, June 19, 1824; *Vermont Gazette*, June 29, 1824.

63. Staudenraus, *Colonization Society*, 84.

64. *New York Commercial Advertiser*, June 21, 1824; Granville, *Biographie*, 120–122.

65. *New York Commercial Advertiser*, July 9, 1824; Granville, *Biographie*, 144–146.

66. *New York Commercial Advertiser*, July 9, 1824; Granville, *Biographie*, 144–146.

67. *Niles' Weekly Register*, July 3, 1824.

68. *Genius of Universal Emancipation*, January 1825.

69. *National Gazette*, June 22, 1824.

70. *Niles' Weekly Register*, June 26, 1824.

71. *Niles' Weekly Register*, July 3, 1824.

72. *Poulson's American Daily Advertiser*, October 15, 1824.
73. *New Bedford Mercury*, November 26, 1824.
74. *Genius of Universal Emancipation*, February 1825.
75. *Genius of Universal Emancipation*, November 1824.
76. Staudenraus, *Colonization Society*, 86.
77. Ibid., 100.
78. "Gottfried Duden's 'Report,' 1824–1827," translated by William G. Bek, *Missouri Historical Review* 13 (1919): 44–56, provides a transcription and summary of most of the letters. A translated version is also available: Gottfried Duden, *Report on a Journey to the Western States of North America*, ed. and trans. James W. Goodrich (Columbia: State Historical Society of Missouri and the University of Missouri Press, 1980).
79. For reports contradicting these rumors, see the website created by Michael Stephenson, *Irish Emigrants in Petersborough*, 2007, http://www.ontariogenealogy.com/peterborough/robinsonemigrants.html (accessed July 6, 2013).
80. Mark. G. McGowan, "Irish Catholics," in *Encyclopedia of Canada's Peoples*, ed. Paul Robert Magocsi (Toronto: University of Toronto Press, 1999), 742.
81. Wendy Cameron, Sheila Haines, Mary McDougall Maude, introduction to *English Immigrant Voices*, xix–xx.
82. Ibid., xxvii, xxxi.
83. The editors of *English Immigrant Voices* discuss the editing process and the different methods used by Sockett in selecting letters for publication (ibid., xxxvi).
84. Sockett, quoted in ibid., xxxv–xxxvi.
85. Because of the mediated nature of published letters, some historians will only use manuscript letters. See David Fitzpatrick, *Oceans of Consolation: Personal Accounts of Irish Migration to Australia* (Ithaca: Cornell University Press, 1994), 26–27; as well as Charlotte Erickson, *Invisible Immigrants: The Adaptation of English and Scottish Immigrants in Nineteenth-Century America* (Ithaca: Cornell University Press, 1990), 3–4. Most historians will use letters published in newspapers but make an effort to discuss the drawbacks and challenges of this type of source.
86. *New York American*, June 21, 1824.

Notes to Chapter 5

1. Although some historians have pointed out the limits to the use of the "push" and "pull" factors that influenced migrants, for most historians who examine migration, this model continues to be the best method for organizing and describing motives. See Bernard Bailyn's introduction to *Europeans on the Move: Studies on European Migration, 1500–1800*, ed. Nicholas Canny (Oxford, UK: Clarendon, 1994), 5, for his discussion on the limits of this model. See Peter C. Meilaender, *Toward a Theory of Immigration* (New York: Palgrave, 2001), 196n. 18, for why it is still a useful organizing model.
2. Historians generally define black nationalism as a separatist ideology that took hold in the African American community in the 1850s. Some historians have claimed that African Americans by aspiring to form a black nation were declaring that they no longer wished to integrate into American society or culture. John H. Bracey, August Meir, and Elliot Rudwick, eds., *Black Nationalism in America*

(Indianapolis: Bobbs-Merrill, 1970); Wilson Moses, *Afrotopia: The Roots of African American Popular History* (New York: Cambridge University Press, 1998), chaps. 2 and 3; Moses, *Golden Age of Black Nationalism, 1850–1925* (Hamden, Conn.: Archon, 1978), 25; Sterling Stuckey, *Slave Culture: The Foundations of Nationalist Thought* (New York: Oxford University Press, 1987), chap. 1. Recently, historians have moved past this dichotomy and viewed black nationalism as an evolving idea that reflected the complex goals, forces, and ideologies shaping the community's views of nation, separation, and migration. Eddie S. Glaude, *Exodus: Religion, Race, and Nation in Early Nineteenth-Century Black America* (Chicago: University of Chicago Press, 2000); Peter Hinks, ed., *David Walker's Appeal to the Coloured Citizens of the World* (University Park: Pennsylvania State University Press, 2000); James Sidbury, *Becoming African in America: Race and Nation in the Early Black Atlantic* (New York: Oxford University Press, 2007); Dickson Bruce, Jr., "National Identity and African-American Colonization, 1773–1817," *Historian* 58 (1995): 15–29.

3. Emigrants came from all over, including Ohio; Richmond, Virginia; Providence, Rhode Island; and the states of New Jersey and Maine.

4. The Haitian Revolution brought in a number of émigrés, both white and black, into all these cities, with the exception of Boston. The great influx of immigrants from Europe, specifically from Ireland and Germany, had started in the 1810s in Philadelphia but faltered during the 1820s. Immigration from Europe was still sizeable in New York during this period.

5. Samuel Rezneck, "Depression of 1819–1822: A Social History," *American Historical Review* 39 (1933): 31.

6. Ibid.

7. Baltimore did not receive large numbers of European immigrants until the 1840s.

8. Donald R. Adams, Jr., "Wage Rates in the Early National Period: Philadelphia, 1785–1830," *Journal of Economic History* 28 (1968): 406, table 1.

9. Sean Wilentz, *Chants Democratic: New York City and the Rise of American Working Class, 1788–1850* (New York: Oxford University Press, 2004), 107.

10. James Oliver Horton and Lois Horton, *In Hope of Liberty: Culture, Community, and Protest among Northern Free Blacks, 1700–1860* (New York: Oxford University Press, 1998), 117–118; Noel Ignatiev, *How the Irish Became White* (New York: Routledge, 1995), 100–102.

11. Charlotte Erickson, *Invisible Immigrants: The Adaptation of English and Scottish Immigrants in Nineteenth-Century America* (Ithaca: Cornell University Press, 1990).

12. Gary Nash, *Forging Freedom: The Formation of Philadelphia's Black Community, 1720–1840* (Cambridge: Harvard University Press, 1988), 180–182 (quote on 182).

13. Mack Walker, *Germany and the Emigration, 1816–1885* (Cambridge: Harvard University Press, 1964), 22.

14. Quoted in ibid., 24.

15. "Irish Potato Famine: Before the Famine," *The History Place*, 2000, http://www.historyplace.com/worldhistory/famine/before.htm.

16. Historians examining these early decades argue that the island's lack of industry—there were no mills (either textile or granaries), naval yards, or extensive manufacturing of any kind—limited and prevented Haiti from breaking the grip of exporting crops held over from its colonial economic system. Historians and contemporaries of the time cited Haiti's refusal to allow any foreigners to own land as limiting its capital accumulation and movement into a mature capitalist society. For example, see Alex Dupuy, *Haiti in the World Economy: Class, Race, and Underdevelopment since 1700* (Boulder, Colo.: Westview, 1989); James Graham Leyburn, *The Haitian People* (New Haven: Yale University Press, 1966).

17. Society for Haytian Emigration, *Information for the Free People of Colour Who Are Inclined to Emigrate to Hayti* (New York: Mahlon Day, 1824); Haytien Emigration Society for Colored People, *Information for the Free People of Colour* (Philadelphia: J. H. Cunningham, 1825); Loring Dewey, *Correspondence Relative to the Emigration to Hayti, of the Free People of Colour, in the United States; Together with the Instructions to the Agent Sent Out by President Boyer* (New York: Mahlon Day, 1824); *United States Gazette*, March 1, 1825; *Vermont Gazette*, June 29, 1824; *New York Observer*, July 16, 1825; *Genius of Universal Emancipation*, March 1825.

18. Elizabeth Jane Errington, *Emigrant Worlds: Migration to Upper Canada in the First Half of the Nineteenth Century* (Montreal: McGill-Queens University Press, 2007), 29.

19. Whether Mrs. Baldwin worked to supplement the family's income remains unknown. Although the average property owned by an African American living in New York is unknown, in 1825, only 68 members of the community of 12,559 met the residency and $250 property requirement for voting. George E. Walker, *The Afro-American in New York City, 1827–1860* (New York: Garland, 1993), 116.

20. Serena Baldwin wrote a letter to her teacher Eliza J. Cox of the African Free School, New York, on September 29, 1824. It can be found in the *United States Gazette*, November 11, 1824; and *Poulson's American Daily Advertiser*, November 11, 1824.

21. *New York City Directory*, 1824.

22. Shane White, in "The Death of James Johnson," *American Quarterly* 51 (1999): 753–795, discusses the entertainment culture that oyster houses promoted.

23. Serena had learned how to read and write during her time at the African Free School for girls, located on William Street, where girls learned reading, penmanship, arithmetic, grammar, geography, and needlework.

24. Francis Lieber, quoted in Ofelia García, "New York's Multilingualism: World Languages and Their Role in a U.S. City," in *The Multilingual Apple: Languages in New York City*, ed. Ofelia García and Joshua A. Fishman, 2nd ed. (New York: Mouton de Gruyter, 1997), 22.

25. W. Jeffrey Bolster, *Black Jacks: African American Seamen in the Age of Sail* (Cambridge: Harvard University Press, 1997), 145.

26. *Niles' Weekly Register*, August 7, 1824.

27. *Le Constitutionnel*, July 28, 1824; *Journal des Debats*, July 15, 1824; *Le Telegraphe*, October 9, 1824; *Niles' Weekly Register*, May 22, 1824; *United States Gazette*, November 4, 1824.

28. Jonathas Henri Théodore Granville, *Biographie de Jonathas Granville par son fils* (Paris: E. Brière, 1873), 120–122; *New York Commercial Advertiser*, June 21, 1824.

29. *Niles' Weekly Register*, April 20, 1822.

30. *Le Telegraphe*, September 26, 1824; *Le Telegraphe*, October 3, 1824.

31. *Niles' Weekly Register*, May 22, 1824; *United States Gazette*, June 10, 1824.

32. *Le Telegraphe*, October 9, 1824; *Journal des Debats*, July 15 and July 29, 1824; *United States Gazette*, November 5, 1824.

33. *Le Telegraphe*, October 9, 1824; *National Gazette*, November 4 and June 3, 1824; *New York Daily Advertiser*, May 31, 1824.

34. This was the situation in one of the city's largest shipyards, owned by Joseph Despeaux. Christopher Phillips, *Freedom's Port: The African American Community of Baltimore, 1790–1860* (Urbana: University of Illinois Press, 1997), 79. Caulking was dominated by free black workers. In the 1822 *Baltimore City Directory*, nineteen of the twenty caulkers listed were free blacks (ibid., 78).

35. Frederick Douglass, *Life and Times of Frederick Douglass*, in *Autobiographies*, ed. Henry Louis Gates, Jr., 453–1045 (New York: Library Classics of the United States, 1995), 628.

36. Ibid., 630.

37. Dewey, *Correspondence*, 25; Granville, *Biographie*, 231; Julie Winch, *A Gentleman of Color: The Life of James Forten* (New York: Oxford University Press, 2002), 218.

38. M. Anderson sailed on the *Stephen Gerard* from Port-au-Prince to Philadelphia, November 18, 1825; J. Newport sailed on the *Mary* from Port-au-Prince to Philadelphia, March 31, 1825. "Passenger Lists of Vessels Arriving at Philadelphia, PA, 1800–1882," National Archives Microfilm Publication M425, National Archives and Records Service, General Services Administration, Washington, D.C., 1958. Francis Mitchell was mentioned in a letter by fellow emigrant John Cromwell. *United States Gazette*, April 5, 1825.

39. Winch, *A Gentleman of Color*, 83.

40. Loring Dewey to Daniel Raymond, *Genius of Universal Emancipation*, May 1825.

41. *Poulson's American Daily Advertiser*, February 10, 1825.

42. *United States Gazette*, November 5, 1824.

43. *United States Gazette*, December 23, 1824.

44. Haytien Emigration Society for Colored People, *Information for the Free People of Colour*, 6.

45. Of course, not all emigrants were attracted to Haiti to prove their military prowess. The Ohio group that was sent to Haiti by George Flowers praised Boyer for giving them exemptions from military duty for one year. *Genius of Universal Emancipation*, October 1824.

46. *United States Gazette*, September 23, 1824.

47. New York State's Gradual Emancipation Laws gave freedom to all slaves born after July 4, 1799, at the age of twenty-eight for males and twenty-five for females. Reed, who was twenty-six years old in 1825, may have been an educated slave who had negotiated his freedom early. For a thorough examination of this

period in New York history, see David Gellman, *Emancipating New York: The Politics of Slavery and Freedom, 1777–1827* (Baton Rouge: Louisiana State University Press, 2006); Shane White, *Somewhat Independent: The End of Slavery in New York City, 1770–1810* (Athens: University of Georgia Press, 1991); Leslie M. Harris, *In the Shadow of Slavery: African Americans in New York City, 1626–1863* (Chicago: University of Chicago Press, 2003).

48. *New York American*, November 29, 1824. Prince Saunders, who had worked in Christophe's government, was another example of an educated African American who had gone to Haiti to become a government minister.

49. John Whitcomb and Claire Whitcomb, *Real Life at the White House: 200 Years of Daily Life at America's Most Famous Residence* (New York: Routledge, 2002), 16.

50. See letters by Arthur J. Jones and George Jann in *Genius of Universal Emancipation*, October 1824.

51. More than 244 females over the age of fourteen appeared on the Passenger Lists from Haitian ports.

52. Quincy returned to New York on the *Robert Y. Haynes*, July 3, 1827. "Passenger Lists of Vessels Arriving at New York, NY, 1820–1897," National Archives Microfilm Publication M237, National Archives and Records Service, General Services Administration, Washington, D.C., 1958.

53. Although no estimates exist for how many women worked as laundresses in New York City, it is likely that, as in Baltimore, more than 60 percent worked in this capacity (Phillips, *Freedom's Port*, 111, table 13).

54. *Niles' Weekly Register*, July 3, 1824.

55. Ibid.

56. For a discussion of women's many contributions to the United States after the American Revolution, see Linda Kerber, *Women of the Republic: Intellect and Ideology in Revolutionary America* (Chapel Hill: University of North Carolina Press, 1980).

57. Harris, *In the Shadow of Slavery*, 74. Perhaps these observers were unaware of Haiti's gender ratio: by some estimates, women there outnumbered men three to one.

58. *Niles' Weekly Register*, July 3, 1824; *Genius of Universal Emancipation*, November 1824.

59. Errington, *Emigrant Worlds*, 32–34.

60. *United States Gazette*, December 23, 1824.

61. *United States Gazette*, April 16, 1825, emphasis in original. These quotes derive from the published proceedings of the Philanthropic Society of Hayti, an organization created to promote and assist in African American migration to Haiti.

62. James Sidbury, in *Becoming African in America*, traces the uses and meanings of "African" among Anglophone populations and argues that blood and historical understandings of kinship were important to creating this identity.

63. *Genius of Universal Emancipation*, July 1825. Fisher, however, was not appealing to the essentialist idea of difference but to the shared goal of a black nation for all people of African descent.

64. According to one observer, a tailor had become a "merchant-taylor" by 1820, a profession that needed at least $2,000 to open a shop in New York City. Richard Brigg Stott, *Workers in the Metropolis: Class, Ethnicity, and Youth in Antebellum New York City* (Ithaca: Cornell University Press, 1990), 36.

65. For a thorough book-length biography of Richard Allen, see Richard Newman, *Freedom's Prophet: Richard Allen, the AME Church, and the Black Founding Fathers* (New York: NYU Press, 2008).

66. The free produce movement did not become formally organized into the Free Produce Society until 1826. Individuals, however, had been boycotting slave-produced goods prior to the society's establishment.

67. Carol V. R. George, *Segregated Sabbaths: Richard Allen and the Emergence of the Independent Black Churches, 1760–1840* (New York: Oxford University Press, 1973), 132. Neither George nor Ruth Nuermberger indicate whether this apparel looked different or distinctive. Nuermberger, *The Free Produce Movement: A Quaker Protest against Slavery* (Durham: Duke University Press, 1942).

68. *United States Gazette*, December 23, 1824.

69. The idea of marketing products as "free labor" is similar to how "organic" is used today on products to sell them to environmentally conscious individuals. Ready-made clothing was in its infancy during the 1810s and 1820s. A few "clothiers" had established themselves in New York City and were making enormous profits. One man, Henry Brooks, the father of the famous Brooks Brothers Company, opened a grocery store on Cherry Street and expanded into the ready-made clothing business in the late 1810s. By the 1820s, he was making over $50,000 a year. Michael Zackim, "A Ready-Made Business: The Birth of the Clothing Industry in America," *Business History Review* 73 (1999): 61–90.

70. Granville's account of Haiti, published with Haytien Emigration Society for Colored People, *Information for the Free People of Colour*, 11.

71. The idea of cultivating cotton in Haiti to compete with American cotton producers did not end with the 1820s effort. James Redpath in the 1860s renewed this idea and made plans to supply free labor cotton, sugar, and tobacco. See Willis B. Boyd, "James Redpath and American Negro Colonization in Haiti, 1860–1862," *Americas* 12 (1955): 173.

72. "Le Marché D'Esclaves: Le principe est établi clairement et distinctement que la marché d'esclaves *doit être abolio*, où bien la traite des esclaves ne sera jamais detruit. Il est aussi vrai de dire que si les acheteurs de coton et de sucre bornaieut leurs spéculations aux articles qui praviennent exclusivement d'un travail libre, le systeme de l'esclave serai bientôt rejeté." *Le Propagateur*, September 1826, 11.

73. Although wheat production had grown significantly during this period in Virginia and Maryland, tobacco continued to be grown.

74. "No. 10, Mackenzie to Canning" (extract), Enclosure C, Minor Articles of Exports from Hayti 1822 to 1826, November 30, 1826, in *British and Foreign State Papers, 1828–1829*, 2 vols. (London, 1831), 2:683.

75. John Sommersett from Philadelphia was also a cigar maker by trade, and he too migrated to Haiti in 1824. On Sommersett's work in the United States, see Nash, *Forging Freedom*, 239.

76. Nash, *Forging Freedom*; Phillips, *Freedom's Port*; White, *Somewhat More Independent*.

77. Although there are no works that focus on northern free black rural life, two works that discuss free black rural life in the Upper South are Reginald Dennin Butler, "Evolution of a Rural Free Black Community: Goochland County, Virginia, 1728–1832" (Ph.D. diss., Johns Hopkins University, 1989); and Michael L. Nicholls, "Passing through This Troublesome World: Free Blacks in the Early Southside," *Virginia Magazine of History and Biography* 92 (1984): 50–70.

78. Adam Hodgson, *Remarks during a Journey through North America in the Years 1819, 1820, and 1821, in a Series of Letters* (1823; repr., New York: Greenwood, 1970), 45–46.

79. Ibid., 46.

80. The Butlers traveled on the brig *Stephen Gerard*, departing from Port-au-Prince and arriving in Philadelphia, May 28, 1825. "Passenger Lists of Vessels Arriving at Philadelphia, PA, 1800–1882."

81. *United States Gazette*, March 1, 1825.

82. This meant that the land, if sold in Philadelphia, was worth $7,200.

83. *United States Gazette*, December 25, 1824.

84. *Vermont Gazette*, March 22, 1825.

85. *Genius of Universal Emancipation*, January 1825.

86. *Poulson's American Daily Advertiser* January 15, 1825.

87. *New York American*, February 22, 1825.

88. Ibid.

89. *Vermont Gazette*, March 22, 1825; *United States Gazette*, March 1, 1825.

90. *New York Observer*, February 26, 1825.

91. Gottfried Duden, *Report on a Journey to the Western States of North America*, ed. and trans. James W. Goodrich (Columbia: State Historical Society of Missouri and the University of Missouri Press, 1980); Paul C. Nagel, *The German Migration to Missouri: My Family's Story* (Kansas City, Mo.: Kansas City Star Books, 2002), 54.

92. Mark G. McGowan, "Irish Catholics," in *Encyclopedia of Canada's Peoples*, ed. Paul Robert Magocsi (Toronto: University of Toronto Press, 1999), 742.

93. Richard Neal to "friends and relations," July 20, 1832, in *English Immigrant Voices: Labourers' Letters from Upper Canada in the 1830s*, ed. Wendy Cameron, Sheila Haines, and Mary McDougall Maude (Montreal: McGill-Queens University Press, 2000), 17.

94. Stephen Goatcher to Elizabeth Burchill, July 6, 1832, in ibid., 15.

95. Neal to "friends and relations," 17–18.

96. Goatcher to Burchill, 16.

97. Neal to "friends and relations," 17.

98. *New York American*, February 22, 1825; *Vermont Gazette*, March 22, 1825. One newspaper calculated that it would bring $1,560. *New York Observer*, February 26, 1825.

99. In Philadelphia, families living in the neighborhoods of Southwark, Moyamensing, and Cedar Ward, where two-thirds of the city's African American community lived, held property worth an average of $165 (Nash, *Forging Freedom*,

248). In Baltimore, the average black property holder in 1815 owned property worth $150 (Phillips, *Freedom's Port*, 98). In New York, 68 out of 12,559 of the city's black residents owned property worth more than $250. George E. Walker, *The Afro-American in New York City, 1827–1860* (New York: Garland, 1993), 116.

100. *Vermont Gazette*, March 22, 1825.

101. *United States Gazette*, March 1, 1825.

102. Ibid.

103. Edward Anderson traveled on the brig *Robert Reade* from Port-au-Prince, arriving in New York City on April 12, 1825. "Passenger Lists of Vessels Arriving at New York, NY, 1820–1897." Ann Holland traveled on the schooner *Richmond* from Port-au-Prince, arriving in Philadelphia on August 6, 1827. "Passenger Lists of Vessels Arriving at Philadelphia, PA, 1800–1882."

104. Boyer gave tax exemptions for one year to Americans who pursued mercantile activities (Dewey, *Correspondence*, 9). For a wholesaler, this amounted to 150 gourdes (Haitian dollars), and for a merchant, 300 gourdes in 1825. Baron S. Linstant, *Recueil général des lois et actes du gouvernement d'Haïti, depuis la proclamation de son indépendance jusqu'à nos jours*, 5 vols. (Paris: Auguste Durand, 1851–1860), 4:174, 4:180. The only Haitian workers exempt from the patent tax included farmers, public or military employees, and hired day laborers or domestic workers. Every other worker in Haiti was required to pay a patent tax, from carters to fishermen. Foreigners, usually merchants, were also required to pay the patent tax, but they were charged a premium, sometimes thousands of dollars for the privilege of working in Haiti (see ibid., 4:170–183, for the entire list).

105. Throughout this period, community professionals—ministers, teachers, publishers—often worked second jobs to support themselves. Hughes quoted in Arthur Truman Boyer, *Brief Historic Sketch of the First African Presbyterian Church of Philadelphia, Pa.* (Philadelphia, 1944), 84. Boyer claims that Hughes left the city and even the country and spent the rest of his life in Africa. There is an advertisement in the October 19, 1827, edition of *Freedom's Journal* from a B. F. Hughes advertising "Evening School" to be held at St. Philip's Church in New York City.

106. *New York Observer*, December 18, 1824. The society was $6,000 in debt and probably could not even pay Hughes's passage.

107. Boyer allowed for private religious worship, but would not allow missionary work. Public disturbances had broken out between Protestant missionaries and Catholics in Port-au-Prince in the early days of Boyer's presidency, and he did not want these repeated. Leslie Griffiths, *A History of Methodism in Haiti* (Port-au-Prince: Imprimerie Méthodiste, 1991), 27–28.

108. A group of New York Presbyterians ventured to Haiti in the summer of 1824. *Western Luminary*, December 8, 1824.

109. *National Gazette*, September 13, 1823; *Le Propagateur*, August 1, 1823.

110. *New York American*, February 22, 1825.

Notes to Chapter 6

1. *Genius of Universal Emancipation*, August 1825.

2. "Pleasance" was the spelling used in the *New York Observer*, July 16, 1825.

3. *United States Gazette*, September 23, 1824.

4. *United States Gazette*, February 16 and June 10, 1824; *Niles' Weekly Register*, May 22, 1824; *New York Daily Advertiser*, May 31, 1824; *National Gazette*, June 3, 1824.

5. Cape Haitian, Port-au-Prince, Santo Domingo, and Port-au-Plat were each to receive about one thousand emigrants. Jeremie, Jacmel, Aux Cayes, and Samana were to receive between two hundred and five hundred emigrants. Boyer relied on American ship captains to transport the emigrants, who may have ignored directives. Loring Dewey, *Correspondence Relative to the Emigration to Hayti, of the Free People of Colour, in the United States; Together with the Instructions to the Agent Sent Out by President Boyer* (New York: Mahlon Day, 1824), 27.

6. *New York Observer*, June 19 and July 9, 1824; *Connecticut Courant*, June 29, 1824.

7. Americans who came to work as sharecroppers or as artisans or merchants were obliged to repay the cost of their passage.

8. *United States Gazette*, January 19, 1825; *Genius of Universal Emancipation*, January 1825.

9. *Baltimore Patriot*, March 10, 1826.

10. *Genius of Universal Emancipation*, March 1825.

11. *United States Gazette*, January 19, 1825.

12. *United States Gazette*, January 19, 1825; *Genius of Universal Emancipation*, January 1825.

13. *Poulson's American Daily Advertiser*, January 11, 1825.

14. *New York Observer*, April 16, 1825.

15. *New York Observer*, July 8, 1825.

16. In the National Archives Passenger Lists, this is their designated occupation.

17. *New York Observer*, July 23, 1825.

18. *New York Observer*, May 10, 1825.

19. *National Gazette*, July 7, 1825; James E. Brice to Henry Clay, October 20, 1825, U.S. State Department Consular Despatches, Cape Haitien Series, vol. 4.

20. *Baltimore Patriot*, December 18, 1824, taken from the *Philadelphia National Gazette*.

21. On Port-au-Prince estimates, see *Rhode Island Republican*, April 27, 1826; for Cape Haitian, see Brice to Clay, March 13, 1826, U.S. State Department Consular Despatches, Cape Haitien, vol. 4.

22. *Christian Journal and Literary Register*, March 1825.

23. *Philadelphia Journal of the Medical and Physical Sciences*, January 1, 1824.

24. Elizabeth Fenn, *Pox Americana: The Great Small Pox Epidemic of 1775–1782* (New York: Hill and Wang, 2001).

25. *Genius of Universal Emancipation*, June 1825; *New York Observer*, July 8, 1825.

26. Prince Saunders had been one of the primary vaccinators, bringing the vaccine from England. Arthur O. White, "Prince Saunders: An Instance of Social Mobility among Antebellum New England Blacks," *Journal of Negro History* 60 (1975): 529.

27. *Portsmouth Journal of Literature and Politics*, July 16, 1825.

28. *New Bedford Mercury*, June 3, 1825; *New York Observer*, July 9, 1825.

29. The Butlers left Port-au-Prince on the *Stephen Gerard* on May 28, 1825. "Passenger Lists of Vessels Arriving at Philadelphia, PA, 1800–1882," National Archives Microfilm Publication M425, National Archives and Records Service, General Services Administration, Washington, D.C., 1958. The Connors and Paschals sailed on the *Robert Reade* for New York City on April 12, 1825. "Passenger Lists of Vessels Arriving at New York, NY, 1820–1897," National Archives Microfilm Publication M237, National Archives and Records Service, General Services Administration, Washington, D.C., 1958.

30. *Genius of Universal Emancipation*, June 1825.

31. *Genius of Universal Emancipation*, March 1825.

32. *United States Gazette*, April 5, 1825.

33. *United States Gazette*, April 5, 1825. John Cromwell reports all of this information in his letter to Richard Allen, dated January 14, 1825, and printed in the *United States Gazette*. I have been unable to obtain further information on Cromwell. Philip Bell may have been the husband of Eliza Bell, who was from Richmond, Virginia, and returned to New York in November 1825, or he may have been the Philip A. Bell who was the New York agent for William Lloyd Garrison's *Liberator*. See Charles A. Wesley, "The Negro in the Organization of Abolition," *Phylon* 12 (1941): 224. There is no further information concerning Thomas Robertson or Francis Duperton. Francie Mitchell may have remained in Samana, as a family of Mitchells living in Samana today can trace their origins back to the 1820s. See E. Valerie Smith, "Early Afro-American Presence on the Island of Hispaniola: A Case Study of the 'Immigrants' of Samana," *Journal of Negro History* 72 (1987): 34, for a list of families who trace their origins in Haiti back to the 1820s.

34. The original offer stood minus paid fares to Haiti: four months of provisions, free land, and the right to work on shares remained. *Le Telegraphe*, June 19, 1825; *Niles' Weekly Register*, June 25, 1825; *Genius of Universal Emancipation*, May 1825; No. 940, "Circulaire du Secrétaire d'État aux administrateurs des arrondissements des Cayes et de Santo-Domingo, concernant la réduction des appointements et du personnel des imprimeries du gouvernement," Port-au-Prince, March 26, 1825, in Baron S. Linstant, *Recueil général des lois et actes du gouvernement d'Haïti, depuis la proclamation de son indépendance jusqu'à nos jours*, 5 vols. (Paris: Auguste Durand, 1851–1860), 4:156.

35. The *Petersburg Intelligencer* and the *National Intelligencer* both printed long articles about Boyer's despotism and the island's unsuitability. The cease-fire between the ACS and Haitian Emigration Society members had broken down. The articles were reprinted in *Genius of Universal Emancipation*, July 4, 1825. Lundy reprinted them to demonstrate the malevolence of the new attacks.

36. *Eastern Argus*, June 13, 1825.

37. *Genius of Universal Emancipation*, May 1825; *Niles' Weekly Register*, June 25, 1825; No. 940, "Circulaire du Secrétaire d'État," 4:156.

38. The signed treaty, which still needed Boyer's and the Haitian legislative approval to be finalized, reached Port-au-Prince in early July 1825. There are different interpretations of how Boyer agreed to this peace treaty. Some historians and contemporaries argue that Boyer was forced to sign the treaty when a large French

fleet accompanied the French ambassador bearing the treaty. See J. N. Leger, *Haiti: Her History and Her Detractors* (1910; repr., Westport, Conn.: Negro University Press, 1970).

39. *United States Gazette*, August 13, 1825.

40. *United States Gazette*, July 29, 1825.

41. *Niles' Weekly Register*, September 1825; *National Gazette*, August 30, 1825; *Genius of Universal Emancipation*, August 1825; Francis Johnson, *Recognition March of the Independence of Hayti* (Philadelphia: F. Willing, 1825).

42. *Eastern Argus*, September 6, 1825.

43. *Niles' Weekly Register*, July 30, 1825.

44. The most thorough discussion of the indemnity talks can be found in Laurent Dubois, *Haiti: The Aftershocks of History* (New York: Metropolitan Books, 2012), chap. 3.

45. There are no diaries or journals written by Boyer.

46. Charles Mackenzie, *Notes on Haiti, Made during a Residence in That Republic*, 2 vols. (London: Henry Colburn and Richard Bentley, 1830), 2:197. The economic and social pressures weighed so heavily on Boyer and Haiti that he commenced mining operations in the former silver and gold mines of the island, but these proved exhausted. *Niles' Weekly Register*, August 19, 1826.

47. *Le Telegraphe*, June 19, 1825; *National Gazette*, September 5, 1825. There were bitter complaints about these new fees by an American merchant living in Cape Haitian. He complained that the "goal of this government is to push foreigners away from the island and destroy their belongings in the process." *National Gazette*, June 7, 1825, quoted in *Le Telegraphe*, June 19, 1825.

48. No. 946, "Loi sur les patentes," Port-au-Prince, April 19, 1825, in Linstant, *Recueil*, 4:170 (pharmacists), 4:176 (doctor). I am using the 1829 exchange rate, which was sixty-seven U.S. cents to one Haitian gourde. *Merchants' Magazine and Commercial Exchange* 41 (1859): 344.

49. B. Burton sailed from Port-au-Plat for Philadelphia on the *Richmond* on December 27, 1825. "Passenger Lists of Vessels Arriving at Philadelphia, PA, 1800–1882."

50. On Spanish demands for compensation, see *National Gazette*, November 17, 1825; on decommissioning troops, see *Friend*, May 28, 1831.

51. Mackenzie, *Notes on Haiti*, 2:181. The drought hit coffee production as well.

52. P. J. Laborie, *The Coffee Planter of Saint Domingo* (London: Printed for T. Cadell & W. Davies, 1798).

53. A price list for coffee from 1820 to 1830 was reprinted in *Niles' Weekly Register*, August 21, 1830.

54. *Jeremie Journal*, 1820–1821, 21.

55. *New York Observer*, July 25, 1825.

56. "No. 3, Mr. Consul-General Mackenzie to Mr. Secretary Canning" (extract), Port-au-Prince, September 9, 1826, in *British and Foreign State Papers, 1828–1829*, 2 vols. (London, 1831), 2:669.

57. *The Rural Code of Haiti* (London: B. McMillan, 1827).

58. Most historians of Haiti see Boyer's Code Rural as the last gasp of presidential power. See Michel-Rolph Trouillot, *Haiti, State against Nation: The Origins and*

Legacy of Duvalierism (New York: Monthly Review Press, 1990), 74; Alex Dupuy, *Haiti in the World Economy: Class, Race, and Underdevelopment since 1700* (Boulder, Colo.: Westview, 1989), 96–97; James Graham Leyburn, *The Haitian People* (New Haven: Yale University Press, 1966), 66.

59. Boyer also implemented more positive incentives. According to Charles Mackenzie, the new May 1 Festival created by Boyer during this period was "to encourage agriculture by the award of prizes to the most successful cultivators" (Mackenzie, *Notes on Haiti*, 1:22). According to Leyburn, Pétion first established this festival (*Haitian People*, 61).

60. Mackenzie, *Notes on Haiti*, 1:60.

61. *Eastern Argus*, August 25, 1826; *National Gazette*, September 6, September 8, and November 19, 1825; *Baltimore American*, April 1, 1828; *United States Gazette*, April 3, 1828.

62. *National Gazette*, March 13, 1826.

63. *National Gazette*, August 11, 1826.

64. Haytien Emigration Society for Colored People, *Information for the Free People of Colour* (Philadelphia: J. H. Cunningham, 1825).

65. *National Gazette*, August 31, 1826.

66. Dewey, *Correspondence*, 27. How the dry conditions brought on by the drought affected the cultivation of the cotton crop also remains unknown.

67. Charles Mackenzie expressed frustration many times about the widely differing numbers and estimates he was given on the cotton crop during his time in Haiti. "No. 18, Mackenzie to the Earl of Dudley" (extract), London, March 31, 1828, in *British and Foreign State Papers*, 2:707, 714.

68. Serena Baldwin wrote to Miss Cox, her African Free School teacher, requesting knitting needles be sent. *United States Gazette*, November 1, 1824; *New York Observer*, July 25, 1825.

69. Money could be had, but it was charged an interest rate of 75 percent. Mackenzie, *Notes on Haiti*, 1:101.

70. These three sailed on the schooner *Horatio* on September 8, 1826. "Passenger Lists of Vessels Arriving at Philadelphia, PA, 1800–1882."

71. Mackenzie, *Notes on Haiti*, 1:43.

72. *National Gazette*, January 27, 1825.

73. Dana F. Minaya, *Freed U.S. Slave Emigrants of 1824 to Samana, Dominican Republic: What Is to Be Learned about Samana History and the African-American Emigrants from the Reports of the 1871 United States Commission of Inquiry?* (Samana, D.R.: Samana College Research Center, 2012).

74. Ibid., 6 (names) and 30 (leaving Samana).

75. Ibid.

76. Ibid., 30.

77. Ibid., 22.

78. Mackenzie, *Notes on Haiti*, 1:110–111; quoted in Julie Winch, *A Gentleman of Color: The Life of James Forten* (New York: Oxford University Press, 2002), 219.

79. *United States Gazette*, February 19, 1827.

80. *Eastern Argus*, June 13, 1828.

81. *Le Telegraphe*, May 7, 1826.

82. Boyer had donated money to assist the first two hundred emigrants back to the United States, but he refused to finance any further returnees' passage. He also remained adamant that settlers who had sailed to Haiti and who had signed a contract to repay the government were still obligated to pay back their passage money.

83. *Eastern Argus*, December 15, 1826.

84. Ibid.

85. *National Gazette*, December 14, 1826.

86. *National Gazette*, December 16, 1826.

87. *National Gazette*, December 28, 1826.

88. Those emigrants who financed their own passage to Haiti were under no obligation to the government and could depart from Haiti when they desired.

89. Rop left Port-au-Prince on February 10, 1828. "Passenger Lists of Vessels Arriving at Philadelphia, PA, 1800–1882."

90. *Baltimore Patriot*, March 10, 1826, originally published in the *Hartford Times*.

91. They left on the schooner *Marquis*, June 7, 1828. "Passenger Lists of Vessels Arriving at Philadelphia, PA, 1800–1882."

92. No records have been found on James Lee's departure. Perhaps he stowed away on a departing ship. Two children, Aug. and Samuel Lee, ages four and six, respectively, sailed from Cape Haitian to Boston on the schooner *Sharn* in April 1826. These may have been Lee's children. No female accompanied them, and they were the only passengers on board.

93. The Baltimore Passenger Lists from 1820 to 1832 were lost.

94. In addition to these women, there were thirty-two women unaccompanied by children who were designated either "Mrs." or "wife" in the National Archives' Passenger List records, and they, too, traveled without a male relative. Interestingly, many of these women traveled together, two or even three on the same ship, suggesting that for some, the return passage may have been an organized event. None of these women were designated a widow.

95. Gary Nash, *Forging Freedom: The Formation of Philadelphia's Black Community, 1720–1840* (Cambridge: Harvard University Press, 1988), 252.

96. The *Mary Ann* left Jeremie, arriving in Philadelphia on April 19, 1827. "Passenger Lists of Vessels Arriving at Philadelphia, PA, 1800–1882."

97. The Gray children sailed on the schooner *Richmond* on August 6, 1827; Peco sailed on the *MacDonough*, arriving in Philadelphia on June 12, 1828; Johnson also sailed on the *MacDonough*, but she arrived in Philadelphia on August 11, 1828. "Passenger Lists of Vessels Arriving at Philadelphia, PA, 1800–1882."

98. They sailed on the brig *Mazzinghi*, which arrived in New York on March 31, 1826. "Passenger Lists of Vessels Arriving at New York, NY, 1820–1897." William Edmonds was mentioned as one of the passengers in the *Poulson's American Daily Advertiser*, September 6, 1824. William Edmonds, age forty-five, a tobacconist, is located on New York City's 1819 Blacks Heads of Household List. For the New York passengers whose occupations were not listed, some hints as to what they did have been attempted by cross-referencing the

Heads of Household List with the Passenger Lists: the seamstress E. Joseph[s] may have been a widow who lived on Thomas Street; J. Henry may have been either a cookshop worker or a chimney sweep; a sawyer, N. Gome, may have been either the wife or sister to George Gomes, a cooper who lived on Church Street; Sally James, who traveled from Port-au-Prince, may have been a laundress and called Sarah James, who lived on Spruce Street, New York.

99. Mackenzie, *Notes on Haiti*, 1:15–16.

100. John Candler, *Brief Notices of Haiti: With Its Condition, Resources, and Prospects* (London: T. Ward, 1842), 69.

101. The Webbs sailed on the schooner *Cyrus*, which arrived in Philadelphia on November 7, 1826. "Passenger Lists of Vessels Arriving at Philadelphia, PA, 1800–1882."

102. They sailed on the brig *Lark*, which arrived in New York on June 6, 1828. "Passenger Lists of Vessels Arriving at New York, NY, 1820–1897." William Baldwin, designated as a "coloured," is listed in the *New York City Directory* for 1830–1831 on Mulberry Street but disappears thereafter from any future directories.

103. Mackenzie described Santo Domingo as having more "internal traffic . . . than in most towns in Haiti" (*Notes on Haiti*, 1:268).

104. Mackenzie, *Notes on Haiti*, 2:179.

105. The two exceptions were St. Thomas and Curaçao.

106. Benjamin Hunt, *Remarks on Hayti as a Place of Settlement for Afric-Americans; and on the Mulatto as a Race for the Tropics* (Philadelphia: T. B. Pugh, 1860), 6.

107. Wilmot-Horton followed up on his migrants by having them answer questions about the number of acres cleared, head of livestock raised, and amount of wheat harvested. He also inquired about the level of satisfaction with the amount of government assistance and how the migrants felt at different points of their move. For more about the papers and sources available on Wilmot-Horton and the Irish migration to Upper Canada, see "Projects," Peannairi web forum, http://peannairi.com/texts/. Scholars that study the Petworth Committee also conclude that the migrants were fortunate to have such organizers to help them. See Wendy Cameron, Sheila Haines, and Mary McDougall Maude, introduction to *English Immigrant Voices: Labourers' Letters from Upper Canada in the 1830s*, ed. Wendy Cameron, Sheila Haines, and Mary McDougall Maude, xv–li (Montreal: McGill-Queens University Press, 2000).

108. *Friend*, October 22, 1831.

109. *United States Gazette*, January 19, 1825; *Genius of Universal Emancipation*, January 1825, 58. In one emigrant account, there was mention of a plough in sharecropper agreements David Barry Gaspar, "Sugar Cultivation and Slave Life in Antigua before 1800," in *Cultivation and Culture: Labor and the Shaping of Slave Life in the Americas*, ed. Ira Berlin and Philip D. Morgan, 101–123 (Charlottesville: University Press of Virginia, 1993), 104.

110. *Friend*, October 22, 1831.

Notes to the Conclusion

1. *New York Observer*, August 20, 1825.
2. Barbara J. Fields, "Ideology and Race in American History," in *Region, Race, and Reconstruction: Essays in Honor of C. Vann Woodward*, ed. J. Morgan Kousser and James McPherson (New York: Oxford University Press, 1982), 143–177.

Index

Abolition/abolitionists: and free labor proposal, 141*n*52; and Haitian emigration, 14, 56, 62, 69; moral suasion as basis of, 127*n*25; and slave trade, 14, 25, 36
ACS. *See* American Colonization Society
Activism, 121
Act of Union (Ireland 1801), 19
Act to Encourage Immigration of 1864 (U.S.), 26
Adams, John, 8, 30
Adams, John Quincy, 51, 52, 138*n*68
Africa as destination for free African Americans, 62, 64–67, 71, 142*n*33
African Americans: acceptance of color as identifier for, 10–11, 129*n*14; criminal convictions of, 80; Panic of 1819's effect on, 78–79; population size in U.S. of, 63; reaction to U.S. conditions of discrimination, 3, 121, 127*n*22; recruitment by Haiti, 1–2, 11, 17–18, 39, 55–57, 62–63, 81–82, 120; rejection of ACS proposal to remove "free colored people," 65; as semiskilled and skilled laborers, 79, 81, 85, 111; voting restrictions on, 80. *See also* Migration to Haiti; Return of Haitian migrants
African Free School (NYC), 83, 86
African Institute, 133*n*61

African Repository and Colonial Journal (ACS), 73
Agriculture, 29, 35, 41, 46, 79, 92–93, 95–96, 102, 105, 112, 155*n*59. *See also* Labor shortage; Plantation system; Sharecropping
Allen, John, 77, 89–91, 109, 110–111
Allen, Richard, 90, 153*n*33
American Colonization Society (ACS): counterattack on Haitian emigration option, 70–71, 73, 153*n*35; defection of members to support Haiti, 56, 63, 68; establishment of, 141*n*22; failure of efforts of, 59; government sponsorship not given to, 21; numbers of migrants to Africa from efforts of, 125*n*2; preference for Africa as relocation destination, 39, 62–68; Richmond free blacks' support for, 142*n*29; southerners as members of, 139*n*83. *See also* Liberian colonization by free African Americans
American Emigrant Company, 26
Anderson, Edward, 96, 151*n*103
Anderson, Moses, 85, 147*n*38
Anticolonial coalition, 2
Apparel industry, 89–90, 110, 149*n*69
Argentina, 27, 51
Armstrong, Andrew, 52

Army, goal of reducing, 35–36, 41, 107, 132*n*46
Arson, 49–50
Australian funding of emigration, 140*n*8

Bacon, Leonard, 67
Bailyn, Bernard, 140*n*5
Baldwin, Serena, 77, 82, 83, 115, 146*n*20, 146*n*23, 155*n*68
Baldwin, William (and family), 77, 82–84, 115–116, 146*n*19
Baltimore: black migration to Haiti from, 86; black population in, 63, 78; Haytian Emigration Society, 67; land ownership in, 92, 151*n*99; Passenger Lists, lack of, 13; shipbuilding industry in, 85; unemployment at Panic of 1819, 46
Baltimore Colonization Society, 142*n*33
Baltimore Patriot on recognition of Haiti, 48
Bell, Philip, 104, 153*n*33
Benton, Thomas Hart, 48
Bernard, J. R., 137*n*50
Betrayal, emigration as, 20
Biassou, Georges, 7
Black identity, 10–11, 129n14
Black nationalism, 3, 144*n*2, 145*n*2
Blandon, Aaron, 99
Bolívar, Simón, 122
Bolster, W. Jeffrey, 49
Boston: migration to Haiti from, 119; return of migrants to, 156*n*92; shipbuilding industry in, 85
Boston African Masonic Lodge, 3–4
Boston Centinel on recognition of Haiti, 50–51
Boston Commercial Gazette on lack of Haitian involvement in Vesey Conspiracy, 53–54
Boston Patriot on lack of Haitian involvement in Vesey Conspiracy, 53–54
Boycott of slave-produced goods, 15, 69, 149*n*66. *See also* Free produce movement
Boyer, Jean-Pierre: ACS's support of Haitian migration plan sought by, 75; biography of, 38–39; conquering and uniting all of Haiti, 44; critical attacks on, citing despotism of, 105, 153*n*35; disappointment with African American immigration to Haiti, 116; and free produce movement, 91; and French recognition, cost of, 84, 105–106, 113; joining revolutionary forces, 9, 28; paying for return trip for migrants back to U.S., 104; reaction to U.S. recognition of Argentina and Columbia, 51; Reed meeting with, 99; resignation called for, 109; seeking African American immigration to Haiti, 1–2, 11, 17–18, 39, 55–57, 62–63, 81–82, 120; seeking U.S. recognition of independent Haiti, 2, 11–12, 14, 15, 99–100, 116, 120; slavery supporters' view of, 54; as successor to Pétion, 38, 39, 41; and Vesey Conspiracy Trials, 53–54, 56. *See also* Indemnity to gain recognition from France; Migration to Haiti
Branagan, Thomas, 142*n*51
Brazil, migration to, 22, 27, 128*n*1
Britain: consular material from 1820s as source, 13; Corn Laws (1817), 46; free produce movement in, 69; invasion at invitation of planters, 7, 131*n*31; migration to Canada, 60–61, 73–74, 82, 94–95, 116, 157*n*107; protection of, sought by Christophe, 35–36; recognition of Haiti sought from, 34–36; slave trade ended by, 36; socioreligious and economic reasons for migration from, 80; trade with Haiti, 32, 131*n*30, 139*n*81; withdrawal after Louverture's rise to power, 7; women's migration from, 88
Brooks, Henry, 149*n*69
Broughman, Lord, 135*n*21
Brown, Jonathan, 130*n*22
Burton, Belfast, 13, 77, 96–97, 106, 154*n*49
Butler, Charles (and family), 77, 91–92, 95, 102, 104, 150*n*80, 153*n*29

Canada: British-assisted migration to, 60–61, 73–74, 94, 157*n*107; depiction of migrant life in, 94–95; difference in emigrants to Canada vs. emigrants to U.S., 80, 88
Cape Haitian, 89, 99, 102, 109, 116, 152*n*5
Cape Mesurado. *See* Liberian colonization by free African Americans

Catholic Association (Ireland), 20
Catholicism: in Haiti, 27, 35, 151*n*107. *See also* Irish migration to U.S.
A Charge to African Masons (Hall), 3
Charleston. *See* Vesey Conspiracy Trials
Christianizing of Africa, 71
Christophe, Henry, 8, 10, 28, 31–37, 132*n*40, 133*n*58
Civil service jobs in U.S., 87
Civil War (U.S.), 26, 122
Clarkson, Thomas, 35, 36, 133*n*58
Clay, Henry, 64
Clothing industry. *See* Apparel industry
Code Henry (Christophe's labor laws), 32, 33, 109
Code Rural (Boyer's labor laws), 108–109, 110, 154*n*58
Code Rural (Pétion's labor laws), 32, 33
Coffee, 5, 31, 32, 33, 81, 93, 95, 99, 107–108
Collins, Charles, 69–70
Colored Haytien Emigration Society of Philadelphia, 109
Columbia, U.S. recognition of, 51
Columbian Republic in South America, 44
Congress, U.S., *Report of the Commission of Inquiry to Santo Domingo* (1871), 111
Congress of Panama (1826), 122
Connor family, 102, 104, 153*n*29
Constitution, Haitian: Christophe's vs. Dessalines's constitution, 133*n*58; color of nation as black, 10, 28; use in soliciting African American migration, 38, 39; voting rights, 112; white landownership outlawed, 10; women omitted from, 129*n*13
Copelain, Daniel, 99
Corn Laws (Britain 1817), 46
Cotton, 90–91, 99, 110, 143*n*53, 155*n*67
Crafts, workers in, 79, 81, 85, 89–90, 110–111, 152*n*7
Criminal punishment: of African Americans in U.S., 80; in Haiti, 109
Cromwell, John, 85, 104, 153*n*33
Cropper, James, 143*n*52
Cuba, 27, 133*n*59
Cuffe, Paul, 37, 63

Darfour, Felix, 50
Debt collection policy, 48–49, 113
Declarations of the Rights of Man and the Citizen, 5

Dei people (Liberia), 66
Depictions of migrant life, 94–95. *See also* Duden, Gottfried
Dessalines, Jean-Jacques, 8, 9, 25, 27–31, 109, 130*n*22, 130*n*25, 131*n*27
Dewey, Loring, 62, 68, 70
Diets of Haitian migrants, 101
Diseases, 65–66, 102–103, 115
Douglass, Frederick, 85, 111
Downing, Thomas, 83
Duden, Gottfried, 60, 73, 93–94
Duperton, Francis, 104, 153*n*33
Dutch independence movement, 42

Eastern Argus on Haitian economic conditions after indemnity agreement with France, 113
Economy: basic economic rights denied to African Americans, 38; Dessalines's plans for lands, 31; and foreign land ownership ban, 146*n*16; indemnity agreement with France weighing on, 113, 154*n*46; migration tied to, 26, 81; Panic of 1819, 46, 136*n*27; Pétion's efforts to stimulate, 33–34; potential of free Haiti, 14. *See also* Indemnity to gain recognition from France; Plantation system; Trade
Edmonds, Clarissa, Eliza, and Lydia, 115
Edmonds, William, 91, 115, 156*n*98
Education program for coffee growers, 95
Egerton, Douglas, 141*n*22
Embargoes: Boyer's embargo of foreign trade, 54–55, 116; Jefferson's embargo of foreign trade, 31, 45–46, 131*n*30, 135*n*19
Empowerment sought by Haitian emigration, 3
England. *See* Britain
Equality. *See* Racial equality/inequality
Erickson, Charlotte, 80
European migration across Atlantic, 18–19, 26–27, 145*n*4

Ferrer, Ada, 133*n*59
Finley, Robert, 64, 141*n*22
Fisher, Charles, 89, 148*n*63
Flour industry, 48
Flowers, George, 148*n*45
Food prices, 101–102, 136*n*28, 136*n*42

Forten, James, 65
Founding fathers of Haiti, 11, 25–39, 120
Fox, Simon, 126n8
France: effort to regain control of St. Domingue after slave revolt (1791), 6–7; grant of equal rights to St. Domingue's free population, 5; invasion threats after Haitian independence, 25–26, 34, 84, 86; Napoleon's attempt to assert control, 8, 28; peace treaty attempts with, 34–35; Pétion negotiating with, 133n62; progress seen by Boyer in attempts to gain recognition of Haiti from, 105; protection to St. Domingue from, 8; refusal to grant recognition, 41, 84, 100, 134n4; slaughter of French in Haiti after independence, 29; in slave trade, 25, 129n1; treaty and indemnity to gain recognition from, 43, 105–106, 109–110, 113, 122, 153n38; withdrawal without formal peace treaty, 9–10, 41
Freehling, William, 56
Free produce movement, 15, 69–70, 90–91, 110, 149n66
French Guyana, 142n50
French Revolutionary principles, 5
Friend (Quaker publication) on Haitian migrant experience, 117–118

Gabriel's Conspiracy, 30, 130n23, 131n26
Geggus, David, 27
Genius of Universal Emancipation (Lundy's newspaper), 12, 62, 66, 123, 153n35
German migration to U.S.: compared to Haitian migration of African Americans, 19, 21–23, 59–60, 82; Duden's promotion of, 19, 21–23, 60, 73, 94–95; effect on African Americans, 79; motivation for, 80–81
Goatcher, Stephen, 94
Golden, Robert, 137n50
Gradual Emancipation Laws (New York), 148n47
Grand'Anse, conquered by Boyer, 43, 45
Grand Lodge of African Freemasonry, 3
Granville, Jonathas, 70, 75, 84, 104
Gray, Patience and Francis, 114–115, 156n97

Great Britain. *See* Britain
Great Famine, 21
Griffith, John, 134n79
Grotius, Hugo, 42
Guadeloupe, 9

Haiti: advertised as black United States, 38; credit rating of, 136n44; cultural differences of population in, 27–28; death rate in, 115; debt payments of, 136n44, 137n51; description of, 1–2; division between North and South, 31–33; founding fathers of, 11, 25–39, 120; instability in, 9–10, 109; as isolated nation, 42–43; name of, 9, 27; proximity to U.S. as factor in opposition to black migration to, 71; symbolism of racial uplift and equality in, 11
Haitian Revolution, 4–5; and advocates for recognition of Haiti, 52; creating fear among U.S. slaveowners, 63; émigrés fleeing to U.S. from, 125n1, 145n4; significance of, 10, 129n2
Hall, Prince, 3–4
Haytian Emigration Society (Baltimore), 67, 134n79
Haytian Emigration Society (New York City), 1, 83–84, 88
Haytian Papers (Christophe's official proclamations and documents), 37
Haytien Emigration Society (Philadelphia), 109
Heyrick, Elizabeth, 143n52
Hicks, Elias, 69–70
Holland, Ann, 96, 151n103
Holly, O. L., 52
Howard (pen name), 51, 52, 138n66
Hughes, Benjamin F., 77, 96, 151n105
Hunt, Benjamin, 125n2
Hutton, Fanny, 88

Indemnity to gain recognition from France, 43, 105–106, 109–110, 113, 122
Industrialization, 79, 136n27, 146n16
Industrial Removal Office, 23
Information for the Free People of Colour (Colored Haytien Emigration Society of Philadelphia), 109
International relations, new era of, 42
Irish migration to Upper Canada, 60–61, 73–74, 94

Irish migration to U.S.: Catholics, 19, 20–21, 81; depiction of, 94; effect on African Americans, 79; as exile, 128*n*7; motivation for, 81; Protestants, 19–20

Jamaica, 131*n*31
James II (king), 81
Jean-François, 7
Jefferson, Thomas, 30, 45, 63, 87, 130*n*23, 130*n*25, 131*n*26
Jewish Immigrant Information Bureau, 23
Jewish migration to U.S., 23
Johnson, Matilda, 115, 156*n*97
Johnson, Michael P., 53, 138*n*70
Jordan, Winthrop, 130*n*23
Jury duty, 112–113

King (ship carpenter), 77, 84–86, 104

Labor laws, 32–33, 108–109, 110, 154*n*58
Labor shortage, 29, 37–38, 81–82
Land ownership: of African Americans in U.S., 91–92, 150*n*99; of African Americans migrating to Haiti, 92–93, 99, 100; foreign land ownership ban, 146*n*16; in Ireland, 81; Pétion distribution of estates to his cronies, 33; redistribution plans of Dessalines, 31; white landownership outlawed in Haiti, 10. *See also* Plantation system
Laundry workers, 87, 148*n*53
Laws of Haiti (1807 to 1833), 14
Le Cap: fire in, 50; and slave revolt (1791), 6
Leclerc, Charles Victor Emmanuel, 8–9, 28
Lee, James (and family), 101, 114, 156*n*92
Letters, use of, 144*n*85
Lewis, Benjamin, 126*n*8
Liberian colonization by free African Americans, 21, 59, 63, 65–66, 68, 71, 73, 125*n*2, 142*n*31. *See also* American Colonization Society (ACS)
"Liberty or Death" speech (Dessalines), 28, 29
Lincoln, Abraham, 26, 123
List, Frederick, 81
Louverture, Toussaint, 7–9, 28, 32, 109, 129*n*3
Lundy, Benjamin: on ACS failure, 66–67; deportation schemes of, 62–63,

140*n*13; and free produce movement, 14, 70; on Haitian independence and progress, 12; and promotion of Haiti, 68, 123; on unrest in Haiti, 50; on whitening of U.S. by Haitian migration, 72, 142*n*46

Mackenzie, Charles, 13–14, 111, 115, 136*n*44, 155*n*59, 155*n*67, 157*n*103
Malaria, 65–66, 115
Manumission, 3, 14, 62
Marketing of Haiti, 59–75, 121; ACS's counterattack on, 70–71; ACS's preference for Africa, 62–68; adverse publicity of return of migrants to U.S., 104; Boyer's incentives to black Americans, 61–62, 70, 82, 92, 120; and free produce movement, 69–70; newspapers advocating for Haitian migration, 62–63, 72
Martinique, 9, 84
Maryland: voting restrictions on free blacks in, 80. *See also* Baltimore
Mercer, Charles Fenton, 64
Migration of Germans. *See* German migration to U.S.
Migration of Irish. *See* Irish migration to Upper Canada; Irish migration to U.S.
Migration to Canada. *See* Canada
Migration to Haiti, 17–23, 77–97; and abolitionists, 14, 56, 62, 69; agricultural opportunities in Haiti, 91–96; backgrounds of migrants, 17, 77–78, 82; coalition formed in U.S. around, 119–120, 122–123; compared to English migration to Canada, 94–95, 116; compared to German migration, 22–23, 59–60, 80–81; compared to Irish migration to U.S., 21, 59, 81; conditions in Haiti discouraging, 101–103; coveted skills by Boyer, 81–82; craftworkers' interest in, 79, 81, 85, 89–90; to cure labor shortage, 29, 37–38, 81–82; description of Haitian migrant experience, 117–118; diets of Haitian migrants, 101; dissatisfaction with and failure of, 109–111, 121; and doctor shortage, 97; economic improvement through, 26; empowerment from, 3; and free produce movement, 69–70

Migration to Haiti (continued)
  incentives offered by Boyer to African Americans, 61–62, 70, 82, 92, 95, 120; incentives withdrawn by Boyer, 104, 153*n*34; lasting effects of, 119, 121; motivations for, 12–13, 17–18, 38, 77, 80, 86, 120; newspaper reports of, 13, 62, 68, 72; Niles as advocate for, 67–68; number of African Americans making, 1; original resettlement plans for, 18; profit motivation for, 96; and recognition of Haiti by U.S., 75, 99–100; repaying cost of passage to Haiti, 100, 152*n*7, 156*n*82; solicitation of African Americans, 1, 11, 17, 36–39; successful stories of, 72, 111–112, 117–118; women as migrants, 87–89, 104. *See also* Return of Haitian migrants
Milroy, John, 137*n*50
Missionaries, 71, 96, 151*n*107
Missouri, German resettlement in, 60, 73, 93–94
Missouri Compromise, 12, 14
Mitchell, Francie, 104, 153*n*33
Mitchell, Francis, 85
Monroe, James, 51, 52, 55
Monroe Doctrine, 2, 55
Mulattos (*gens de couleur*): ouster of Louverture sought by, 8; Pétion as choice to succeed Dessalines, 31; resentment of Dessalines, 28; rights of, 5–6

Napoleon, 8, 28, 34, 60, 131*n*26
Napoleonic Wars, 22, 32, 46, 60, 79, 135*n*19, 140*n*5
National Advocate on African American migration to Haiti, 68
National Archives' Passenger Lists for New York and Philadelphia, 13, 113–114, 156*n*94. *See also* specific cities
National Gazette (Philadelphia): on conquest of Santo Domingo, 45; on Haitian doctor shortage, 97; on Haitian economic crisis, 113; on Haitian migration as boon to national security, 71
National Intelligencer on recognition of Haiti, 53
National Recorder on universal emancipation, 64
Naval treaties, 18

Neal, Richard, 95
Negro Seaman Acts (South Carolina), 138*n*78
Newburyport Herald on Boyer's conquest of Grand'Anse, 44
Newport, John, 85
Newspaper reports: on ACS meeting proposing colonization plans, 68; of Boyer's displeasure of lack of recognition, 55; on Boyer's trade policies, 49, 91; on Boyer's uniting Haiti, 44, 45; on Darfour, 50; on German migration accounts, 60; on Granville's arrival in U.S., 70; on Haitian doctor shortage, 97; on Haitian economic crisis, 113; of Haitian independence and progress, 12; on Haitian migration, 68, 71, 72; of Haitian trade's importance to U.S., 47; on lack of Haitian involvement in Vesey Conspiracy, 53–54; on Liberia as failed experiment, 67–68; on migrants repaying transport costs, 26; promoting African American emigration to Haiti, 13, 62, 68, 72, 92, 95–96; on recognition of Haiti, 48, 50–51, 53; on universal emancipation, 64
New York (state): African American voting rights in, 80, 83; Gradual Emancipation Laws, 148*n*47
New York City: black laundresses in, 87, 148*n*53; black population in, 63–64, 78, 82, 88; cultural demographics of, 83; land ownership in, 151*n*99; migration to Haiti from, 1, 119, 125*n*2; Passenger Lists, 13, 115; return of Haitian migrants to, 115, 151*n*103, 153*n*29, 156*n*98, 157*n*102; shipbuilding industry in, 85; smallpox in, 103; tobacco market in, 91; unemployment at Panic of 1819, 46
New York Commercial Advertiser: ACS campaign against Haiti in, 70–71; on meeting in New York City on ACS's colonization plans, 68
New York Missionary Society, 96
New York Public Library, 14
New York Society for the Prevention of Pauperism, 78
New York Times on migrants repaying transport costs, 26
Niles, Hezekiah, 12, 45, 47, 48, 54, 62–63, 67–68, 70, 71–72, 88

Notes on Haiti (Mackenzie), 13–14
Nuermberger, George and Ruth, 149*n*67

Observations on the Slavery of the Africans and Their Descendants, and on the Use of the Products of Their Labor (Hicks), 69
O'Connell, Daniel, 20, 21
Ogé, Vincent, 5
Ohio, solution to slavery proposed in, 61
Orphan children returning from Haiti to U.S., 114–115

Panic of 1819, 46, 78–79, 91, 135*n*23
Paschal family, 102, 104, 153*n*29
Patent tax. *See* Taxes
Peace of Westphalia (1648), 42
Peco, Joseph, 115, 156*n*97
Penal Laws (Britain), 81
Pennsylvania: voting restrictions on free blacks in, 80. *See also* Philadelphia
Pétion, Alexandre: and army size, 132*n*46; and coffee taxes, 132*n*44; division with other revolutionary leaders, 10, 31–32; Grand'Anse, attempts at conquering, 44; joining Haitian revolt, 9, 28; negotiating with France, 133*n*62; seeking African American migration to Haiti, 37–38; seeking recognition of Haiti from Britain, 34
Petworth Emigration Committee (Britain), 61, 74–75, 82, 94, 116, 157*n*107
Philadelphia: African American population in, 64, 78; African American rejection of ACS's plan in, 65; African American uprising in (1804), 4; land ownership in, 92, 150*n*99; migration to Haiti from, 72, 90, 97, 102, 119; Passenger Lists for, 13, 113–114; return of Haitian migrants to, 151*n*103, 153*n*29, 156*nn*96–97, 157*n*101; shipbuilding industry in, 85; smallpox in, 103; unemployment at Panic of 1819, 46; widowhood of African American women in, 114
Philanthropic Society of Hayti, 148*n*61
Plaisance (Haiti), 99
Plantation system, 26, 32, 108–109
Political motivations for migration to Haiti, 17–18, 38, 61, 121
Polverel, Étienne, 6, 7

Port-au-Plat settlers, 111, 152*n*5
Port-au-Prince: drought in, 101–102, 104, 155*n*66; fires in, 49–50, 137*n*50; migrants returning from, 115; migrants settling in, 99, 100–102, 117–118, 152*n*5; shipping costs, 116; smallpox epidemic in, 102–103; unrest in, 109, 151*n*107; voting rights in, 112
Poulson's American Daily Advertiser on successful migration to Haiti, 72
Poverty, 60, 81, 121
Presbyterians, 96, 151*n*108
Profit motivation for migration to Haiti, 96
Le Propagateur: on Boyer's trade policies, 49, 91; on Boyer's uniting Haiti, 44
Protestants, 35, 112, 151*n*107. *See also* Irish migration to U.S.
Punishment. *See* Criminal punishment
Puritans, 17, 80
Push and pull factors in migration, 77, 144*n*1

Quakers, 143*n*53
Queen of the Antilles, 51–52
Quincy, Hannah, 13, 77, 87–88, 148*n*52

Racial equality/inequality: African American community's rights, 80; Haiti as land of equality, 2, 81–87, 92, 97; Haiti disappointing migrants in, 110, 116; in skilled occupations, 85
Racial fears in U.S.: and Haiti-U.S. relations, 119, 121, 123; marketing Haiti as solution to, 59; of slave revolts, 63; Vesey Conspiracy fueling, 56; voting rights of African Americans, 80
Raimond, Julien, 5
Recognition of independent Haiti: French recognition, 9–10, 43, 84, 100, 105; French withdrawal without declaration of independence, 9–10; lack of, as problem to founding fathers, 25–26, 41–42, 120; opposition within Haiti due to debt collection policy, 48–49. *See also* U.S. recognition as goal for Haiti
Recueil général des lois et actes du gouvernement d'Haïti, 14
Reed, Abel, 77, 86–87, 99, 148*n*47

Religion. *See* Catholicism; Protestants; specific denominations
Report of the Commission of Inquiry to Santo Domingo (U.S. Congress), 111
Report on a Journey to the Western States of North America (Duden), 60, 93–94
Return of Haitian migrants, 99–118; conditions precipitating, 101–104, 116; French indemnity as reason for, 109–110; instability and violence fueling, 109; lack of funds for, 113–114; and migrants who paid own way to Haiti, 156*n*88; numbers of, 103, 122; orphan children, 114–115; payment for return trip paid by Boyer, 104, 156*n*82; tax increases as reason for, 106; women returning, 114
Rigaud, André, 7, 10, 28
R.M.S. (migrant from Philadelphia), 111
Robertson, Thomas, 104, 153*n*33
Rochambeau, Donatien Marie Joseph de, 9
Roman Catholic Relief Act of 1829 (Britain), 20
Rop, William, 114, 156*n*89
Rural life of free African Americans, 78, 92, 150*n*77

St. Domingue, 3, 4, 25, 90, 132*n*36. *See also* Haitian Revolution
Samana (Haiti), 85–86, 97, 99, 104, 111–112, 152*n*5
Santo Domingo: Boyer's conquest of Spanish colony, 44–45; Mackenzie's description of, 157*n*103; settlers in, 83, 111, 152*n*5; Spain seeking compensation for loss of, 106–107. *See also* Samana
Saunders, Prince, 27, 36–37, 133*n*61, 148*n*48, 152*n*26
Schaffer, Johan, 22
Scotch Irish as cultural heritage in U.S., 20
Second jobs, need for, 96, 151*n*105
Self-Accusation Concerning His Travel Report, to Warn against Further Rash Emigration (Duden), 73
Sharecropping, 95–96, 100–101, 107, 152*n*7
Sherbro Island (Africa), 65, 67
Shipbuilding industry, 85, 104, 147*n*34
Ships: *Amelia*, 114; *Cyrus*, 157*n*101; deserting black sailors, 49; *De Witt Clinton*, 115; *Four Sons*, 111; *Horatio*, 155*n*70; *Lark*, 157*n*102; *MacDonough*, 156*n*97; *Marquis*, 156*n*91; *Mary Ann*, 156*n*96; *Mazzinghi*, 156*n*98; *Olive Branch*, 104; *Richmond*, 151*n*103, 156*n*97; *Robert Reade*, 151*n*103, 153*n*29; *Scharn*, 156*n*92; *Stephen Gerard*, 147*n*38, 150*n*80, 153*n*29; to transport migrants, 18–19, 152*n*5
Sidbury, James, 148*n*62
Sierra Leone, British policy on slavery in, 36, 63, 66
Sigel, Franz, 22
Slave revolts: Acul parish (1791), 6. *See also* Gabriel's Conspiracy; Vesey Conspiracy Trials
Slaves: Christophe's offer to buy African slaves captured by British, 36; Dessalines's offer to buy African slaves intended for Jamaica, 30; emancipation declared in U.S., 123; emancipation scheme proposed in Ohio (1824), 61; freedom granted by France to all St. Domingue's slaves, 7; Napoleon's victory reinstating slavery, 9; runaway British slaves to be returned to British, 110; significance of independent black Haiti for, 3, 10, 53, 131*n*26; slave trade, 14, 25, 36, 129*n*1. *See also* Manumission
Slave trade abolition, 14, 25, 36, 71
Smallpox, 102–103, 115
Sockett, Thomas, 61, 74–75
Sommersett, John, 77, 149*n*75
Sonthonax, Léger, 6, 7
South Carolina: Negro Seaman Acts, 138*n*78; Vesey Conspiracy Trials, 12, 52–53
Southern states, U.S.: division over slavery's solution, 56; reaction to Haiti as relocation destination for free blacks, 71; reaction to recognition of Haiti, 48
Spain: demand for compensation to cover loss of Santo Domingo, 107; invasion using slaves as allies for, 6–7; withdrawal after Louverture's rise to power, 7
Spanish American wars of independence, 122, 135*n*19
Spoils system in U.S., 87

Suffrage laws, 80, 81, 112
Sugar production, 29, 31, 32, 33, 81, 90, 117

Tailors, 89–91, 149n64
Taino Arawak name Haiti, 9, 27
Tapsico, Lewis, 65
Tapsico, William, 114
Taxes, 49–50, 106, 151n104
Le Telegraphe (official state newspaper): on Darfour, 50; inattention to African American migration, 116
Thirty Years' War, 42
Thompson, Jeremiah, 143n53
Thoughts on the Colonization of Free Blacks (Finley), 141n22
Tobacco, 91, 95, 149n73
Tobago, 9
Trade: Boyer's embargo, 54–55, 116; Britain's excess wares after Napoleonic Wars, 79; Britain with Haiti, 32, 131n30, 139n81; concessions in exchange for U.S. recognition, 42; drop in Haiti (1824–1826), 108, 116; French slave trade, 25; Jefferson's embargo, 31, 45–46; protective U.S. tariffs (1816), 46; U.S. with Haiti, 8, 30–31, 45–47, 68–69, 116. See also Free produce movement; *specific products*
Treaty. See France
Tredwell, James, 38, 134n67, 134n71
Trinidad, British policy of returning captured slaves to, 36
Tyler-McGraw, Marie, 141n29

Ultra-Royalists party, 133n50
Unemployment after Panic of 1819, 78
United States: Haiti's influence on race relations in, 14, 119–120; migrants arriving in early 19th century, 19; slavery-divided nation's view of Haiti, 11–12. See also African Americans; Migration to Haiti; Return of Haitian migrants; Southern states, U.S.; Trade; U.S. recognition as goal for Haiti
United States Gazette on recognition of independent Haiti, 48
Urban life of free African Americans in U.S., 78, 92
U.S. recognition as goal for Haiti, 2, 11–12, 14, 41–57, 120; achievement of recognition, 122; and African American migration to Haiti, 75, 84, 99–100, 120–121; debate within U.S. over, 43, 121; failure of U.S. to recognize, 105, 116, 122; southern states' reaction to, 48; U.S. trade with Haiti as factor, 45–47

Vaccinations for smallpox, 103, 152n26
Vastey, Baron de, 35–36
Vesey Conspiracy Trials (South Carolina), 12, 52–53, 56, 138n70
Violence rumored in Haiti, discouraging migration, 109
Vodou, 27
Voting rights. See Suffrage laws

Washington, Bushrod, 64
Webb family, 115, 157n101
Webster, Harriet and Rachel, 110–111
Weekly Register. See Niles, Hezekiah
Wesleyans, 112
West Indies slave-revolt scandals, 12
White, Shane, 146n22
Whitening by encouraging nonwhites to migrate, 72, 139n1, 142n46
Whites: dispossessed by Dessalines, 29, 131n27; Haitian citizenship offered to, 36
White supremacy: challenge from American diplomatic ties with Haiti, 2; challenge from Haitian Revolution, 10; as entrenched idea in U.S., 43; rejection by African American community, 127n22. See also Racial fears in U.S.
Wilberforce, William, 35
Williams, Peter, 1–2, 13, 14
Wilmot-Horton, Robert, 60–61, 73, 82, 94, 116, 140nn7–8, 157n107
Women: as migrants to Haiti, 87–89, 104, 148n51, 148nn56–57; omitted from Haitian constitution, 129n13; as returning migrants to U.S., 114, 156n94; widowhood of African American women, 114, 156n94; as workers, 29, 130n19

Yellow fever, 65–66

Zionism, 23

About the Author

Sara Fanning is Assistant Professor of History at Texas Woman's University, where she teaches courses on Haiti, Haitian-U.S. relations, the Caribbean, Latin America, slavery and abolition, and migration studies. She lives in Denton, Texas, with her husband and two daughters.

Early American Places

*Colonization and Its Discontents: Emancipation,
Emigration, and Antislavery in Antebellum Pennsylvania*
Beverly C. Tomek

*Empire at the Periphery: British Colonists, Anglo-Dutch Trade,
and the Development of the British Atlantic, 1621—1713*
Christian J. Koot

*Slavery before Race: Europeans, Africans, and Indians
at Long Island's Sylvester Manor Plantation, 1651–1884*
Katherine Howlett Hayes

*Faithful Bodies: Performing Religion and Race in the Puritan
Atlantic*
Heather Miyano Kopelson

*Against Wind and Tide: The African American Struggle
against the Colonization Movement*
Ousmane K. Power-Greene

*Four Steeples over the City Streets: The Social Worlds of
New York's Early Republic Congregations*
Kyle T. Bulthuis

*Caribbean Crossing: African Americans and the Haitian
Emigration Movement*
Sara Fanning